Pelican Library of Business and Management
Advisory Editor: T. Kempuner

Managers and Magic

Graham Cleverley was born in 1933. After
graduating from Cambridge, where he edited
Varsity, he joined *Picture Post* as a feature
writer. Later he was one of the team – as art
editor – who launched the *Sunday Telegraph*. He
moved further into management, becoming
director of manpower development for I P C,
from which he resigned in 1970. Since then he has
been working as freelance writer – this is his
first book – and occasional consultant. In the
1966 General Election he stood, unsuccessfully,
as a Liberal candidate. He is married and has
three sons.

Managers and Magic

Graham Cleverley

Drawings by John Jensen

Penguin Books

Penguin Books Ltd, Harmondsworth,
Middlesex, England
Penguin Books Australia Ltd, Ringwood,
Victoria, Australia

First published by Longman 1971
Published in Pelican Books 1973

Copyright © Graham Cleverley, 1971

Made and printed in Great Britain by
Richard Clay (The Chaucer Press), Ltd,
Bungay, Suffolk
Set in Linotype Times

Contents

Preface

I don't remember when it first occurred to me. If I had the meticulous kind of mind that keeps track of things, then I suppose I wouldn't have to remember. If a diary was more to me than a device to ensure I don't arrange two lunches in one day more than once a month, I'd be able to find an entry, like maybe:

15 June 196–: Six rubber plants arrived in the office in response to our complaints about static. For insulation?

or:

10 October 196–: Made ineffective attempt at LRPS conference to suggest planning ought to start with finding out what people really want to achieve. Speaker restored order by intoning: 'The purpose of a business is to maximize long-term return on investment.' If that's true, why doesn't anyone try?

or:

14 July 196–: Asked —'s Personnel Director what use his Management Inventory' was to his company. Choleric response indicates he doesn't know. But he knows he's right.

Unfortunately I don't have that kind of mind. Or that kind of diary. So the incident that first made it blindingly clear to me that the majority of managerial time is spent on practices whose only value is ritualistic and magical is lost to posterity.

All I do know is that it must be four or five years since I first threatened to write a book about it. So for all the people I've bored stiff telling them what was going to be in it, here it is.

Introduction

My memories of the Savoy Hotel are all pleasant, though highly varied. Most are irrelevant to my theme, like being too ill to eat anything but oysters and milk and discovering that, even in the Restaurant, the Savoy does not decant its milk but serves it in the bottle. But one is highly pertinent.

I remember a dinner held for the benefit of the head of a rather well-known consulting firm. He was to tell the senior executives of a client company some of the principles on which his consultant teams operated. In particular, he was to explain the progress they had been making in investigating that client's organization. Predictably, his speech went over well. It was helped by his own charm and fluency, as well as the rather good food, and excellent wine, liqueurs and cigars.

Much of what was said now escapes me. I even forget the menu and the wine-list. But what stands out very clearly is the question asked by one of the more likeable and self-confident executives there. 'Mr Chairman,' he asked, 'could Mr — please explain why, whenever he uses the word "people", he does so through clenched teeth?'

The answer I don't remember, except that it was somewhat strained. The question remains and is of some importance to this book. For to me it seems easily understandable that anyone attempting to apply rational principles and thinking to the practice of management should be forced to clench his teeth whenever he is reminded that ultimately he has to deal with people.

People are not rational. Nor are they susceptible to rational control systems. It is a truth that most management writers blindly ignore. Unfortunately, to ignore it is to ensure disaster. To base one's actions on what people ought to be like, rather than what they are like, is suicidal.

I remember a well-known little story about a personnel man-

ager somewhere in the East Midlands. He was summoned to
the shop floor. The shop steward had just told his members to
put their tools down and leave, on the grounds that it was too
cold. Hastily, the personnel manager produced a thermometer.
It read 62 degrees. 'Look,' he argued, 'the temperature is 62
degrees. According to our agreement, you only stop work if it
goes below 60 degrees.'

The steward's rejoinder deserves its subsequent celebration.
'I don't care,' he said. 'What good are 62 degrees on a — cold
day like this?'

The story is normally told from the personnel manager's
point of view as an example of the perverse obduracy of trade
unionists and their disregard of written agreements. But to
treat it in that way is to obscure the real value of the parable.
My sympathies in fact are with the shop steward. What good
are 62 degrees on a — cold day? What matters is what people
feel, not what the thermometer measures. That they 'ought' to
feel warm is of no importance compared to the fact that they
actually feel cold.

Similarly, it is immaterial that people *ought* to pursue
profits, *ought* to be satisfied with a decent wage, *ought* to want
enriched jobs, *ought* to think clearly and rationally, *ought* to
behave consistently with their beliefs. In this book I am totally
unconcerned with what people should be like, whether on
moral grounds or in order to match any of the demands of
business efficiency.

I want to make this perfectly clear because so much of the
literature of management is designed to preach that every book
in the field is automatically assumed to have a didactic purpose. This is the fate, for instance, that befell one of the most
sensible and objective writers about people in organizations, the
late Douglas McGregor. In his book, *The Human Side of
Enterprise*, he coined the terms 'Theory X' and 'Theory Y' and
used them to label two sets of beliefs a manager might hold
about the origins of human behaviour. He pointed out that the
manager's own behaviour would be largely determined by the
particular beliefs that he subscribed to.

It was a simple and sensible thing to do. McGregor hoped
that his book would lead managers to investigate the two sets

of beliefs, invent others, test out the assumptions underlying them, and develop managerial strategies that made sense in terms of those tested views of reality.

But that isn't what happened. Instead, McGregor was interpreted as advocating 'Theory Y' as a new and superior ethic – a set of moral values that *ought* to replace the values managers usually accept. Ironically, both his supporters and his opponents took the same view. And for the past decade the battle between 'X' and 'Y' has been fought out on what, for McGregor, must have been totally the wrong grounds.

In his introduction to McGregor's second book, *The Professional Manager*, published posthumously, Edgar Schein tells of McGregor's attitude to his reception: 'In my own contacts with Doug, I often found him to be discouraged by the degree to which Theory Y has become as monolithic a set of principles as those of Theory X, the over-generalization which Doug was fighting. He wanted Theory Y to be a *realistic* view ... Yet few readers were willing to acknowledge that the content of Doug's book made such a neutral point, or that Doug's own presentation of his point of view was that coldly scientific.'

From McGregor's discouragement, from the failure of his attempt to inject rationality into the way in which managers conduct their business, comes part of the thesis of this book. For his failure is only surprising if one starts from an assumption which is common but highly optimistic. It is the assumption that managers are rational creatures ready to apply empirical and scientific methods in the pursuit of objectively determined goals.

They aren't – with very few exceptions. For myself I don't think I'd be very happy if they were. Yet it is a virtually universal belief that they ought to be. And because of the way in which beliefs about what ought to be are usually transmuted into beliefs about what is, the essential irrationality of managerial behaviour is invariably overlooked and ignored.

Though he wasn't specifically writing about managers, Henri Bergson presented a much truer picture: 'The truth is that if Civilization has profoundly modified Man, it has done so by making the social milieu into a kind of reservoir for accumu-

lating habits and skills which are poured into the individual by
Society ... Scratch the surface and efface what we receive
from an education that never ceases, and we shall discover
something very like primitive humanity in the depths of our
nature ... Human nature is the same today as it has always
been.'

That may sound like a cynical view, an expression of a pro-
found pessimism. I don't think it is. It is only our fashionable
conditioning that makes us think so. We are in the habit of
considering ourselves rational members of a rational culture,
and we believe ourselves therefore superior to the 'primitive'
and 'superstitious' societies from which ours developed. The
facts of our scientific and technical superiority are undeniable;
so is our superior ability to hold together large organizations,
economic or political, and to mobilize resources to achieve our
ends. But progress has by and large been neither because nor in
spite of any major change in man's basic nature. To say that
he is still an irrational being is not therefore to give up hope
that that progress will continue. It may indeed be an expression of faith that it will.

For the moment, however, all I am concerned with is
establishing a *prima facie* case for an investigation of the two
beliefs that provide the theme of this book:

1. Just as he is in any other setting or walk of life, man as
manager is an irrational being.

2. There are illuminating parallels between the behaviour of
managers today and men in the 'superstitious' societies of
earlier days.

Let me run over one or two of the observations that led me to
this point of view.

Not so long ago, one of the convulsions that foreshadowed
the take-over of the International Publishing Corporation was
the dismissal of the chairman, Cecil King. He was replaced by
his deputy, Hugh Cudlipp. I'll have more to say about the
ritual aspects of that event later. The incident that stands out
in my memory is walking into King's old suite of offices a few
weeks after his departure. The whole place had been gutted.
The furniture and decorations had gone. The wall panellings

had been stripped, the floorings lifted, the fireplace pulled out. Even the electric fittings were down to bare wires.

Granted the new chairman had his own ideas about furnishings. But as a couple of us stood there in the bareness, it was evident from the atmosphere that more than a refurnishing was taking place. That alone wouldn't account for the scrupulous meticulousness with which the traces of occupancy had been removed. Nor would it account for the attitudes of the staff. Passing by or looking in, they automatically lowered their voices, as we ourselves were doing, to a church-like hush. It was almost as if a ritual purification were taking place. A little while later I realized that 'almost as if' was too weak a phrase. A ritual purification *had* taken place.

And too many managers have witnessed similar events for it to be dismissed without a little further investigation.

Jumping down several levels from those exalted heights, I also remember an incident from a week's residential course I once went through. Run by the Anne Shaw Organization, it consisted of role-playing exercises in the morning followed by discussion and analysis that tended to go on into the early hours. A fairly standard situation, except that a good deal more money, ingenuity and effort than usual had been expended to achieve verisimilitude, and to open up meaningful learning experiences.

Among other things they supplied secretaries. Which was splendid, except that at the end of the week the secretaries turned round and told us what they thought of us. Politely, but pointedly.

As it happens, I usually reckon myself to be pretty effective at handling women. So I was taken aback to come heavily under fire. Because, *even while I was playing the role of a managing director,* I'd turned up at the 'office' wearing an open-necked jacket-shirt and slacks.

It sounds silly. But the girl concerned had obviously been deeply thrown by this variation from accepted behaviour. Since then I've watched closely whenever I've organized or been involved in a role-playing exercise. One thing stands out very clearly. Any manager who, in such an exercise, is asked to take on a role higher than his accustomed level will automatically

adopt certain behavioural traits which are not accounted for by
the objective situation. Nor, in this role-playing, can they be
accounted for by any fear of what his bosses might think.

What was gradually borne in upon me in making these observations was that managerial behaviour is circumscribed by a
system of taboos – not metaphorically, but actually. Such
taboos get stronger and more powerful the nearer one gets to
the top of the organizational hierarchy. Breaking any one of
them creates unease not only in the violator but in any other
members of the same culture who happen to witness it. So
strong are the taboos – and so irrational – that they are even
carried over into situations where there can be no actual fear
of retribution.

Similar hints and indications are multitudinous in any management situation. It pays, for instance, to think a while about
the habit of asking job applicants for referees. It must be about
the most useless of all the ritual appurtenances of management. Many companies recognize the fact by signing on recruits before their references come in – if they take them up at
all. Yet everybody asks for them. And the shocked reaction I
invariably get when it's discovered that I habitually and gaily
sign on people without at all bothering with references demonstrates that the process is one that people *believe* in. Even if
they are ready to admit that, rationally, it serves no useful
purpose.

It's easy to list endless instances of practices that managers
insist on carrying out, even though they can be driven to admit
that they have no pragmatic validity. How many companies
religiously publish house journals that even their editors will
admit (privately) have no valid function? How many chairmen
ritually visit their factories at periodic intervals, even though
their best friends recognize that, if anything, productivity declines as a result? And how many presentations are ceremonially made by managers who have to be reminded of the name
of the retiring employees they are praising?

I slipped in a few adverbs that probably sounded like metaphors. Religiously, ritually, ceremonially ... In the face of the
evidence that can be found everywhere by anyone who cares to
look, why stop at calling them metaphors? The whole process

becomes much easier to understand and to control as soon as we recognize that what we are confronted with *is* religious in nature, *is* ritualistic, *is* ceremonial, is *magical*.

Magic is a term that it is very difficult to define acceptably. Ernest Crawley makes an attempt in his classic analysis of marriage and courtship customs, *The Mystic Rose*, which may provide a reasonable starting point: 'The primitive mental habit in its general features is best described negatively by the term *unscientific*, and positively by *religious*, in the ordinary connotation of that term. *Superstitious* would be preferable, were it not too narrow; as to *magic*, we do not here distinguish – magic being simply the superstitious or religious *method* as opposed to the scientific.'

Unfortunately, however, in common usage 'magic' is used much more widely, since the term 'religion' is normally used in a much more restricted way than it is by anthropologists. In fact, one of his New York University students once offered George Vetter a definition of religion which would probably serve equally well to define the normal concept of magic. According to this definition religion consists of the 'beliefs that cannot be destroyed by the presentation of contrary evidence, and the practices whose continuance is independent of their efficacy'.

All human behaviour has two kinds of end. It is either directed at influencing and controlling the environment (including other people), or it is directed at releasing some kind of inner conflict, at settling unease or expressing emotion. The first kind I shall be calling *instrumental*, and the second *expressive*. That establishes one reasonably satisfactory set of definitions. I shall be keeping them conceptually separate, even though any one individual act is likely to combine both motivations.

The second dichotomy I will be using is between *scepticism* on the one hand, and *faith* on the other. In non-philosophical language, the sceptic doesn't believe anything unless he can see it positively working. Even then he will drop his current theories for new ones if they can be shown to produce superior results. For him truth is a transient phenomenon. The man who has faith, however, sticks unshakeably to his beliefs irrespective of the 'facts', even to the extent of denying his own senses, as Vetter's definition of religion points out. For him truth is revealed, eternal and unquestionable.

So we have two independent dichotomies, instrumental-expressive and sceptical-credulous. We can easily therefore define four different categories of behaviour, four different approaches to life. I'm going to label them technology, science, magic and religion, even if that may be slightly at variance with everyday usage, and even though some linguistic purists may object. For practical purposes the differences shouldn't matter. In brief:

Technology represents instrumentalism and scepticism. The technologosist is by nature sceptical and concerned with affecting the environment.

Science is also sceptical, but is a form of expressive behaviour. While the scientist is sceptical and open to new thinking as long as it is experimentally verifiable, he is concerned mainly with the establishment of knowledge, with satisfying his and other people's doubts about the world.

Magic is instrumental in nature but dependent on faith. Its practitioners are attempting to influence their environment (real or imagined), but are above such things as evidence or empirical testing.

Religion is also credulous, but is expressive in nature. The religious believer discounts evidence and is mainly concerned with establishing 'truth' and satisfying and expressing emotional impulses that 'come from within'.

Where the confusion between instrumental and expressive behaviour becomes too dense to permit separation, I'll stick to the term *magico-religious*, and hope it's self-explanatory.

The behaviour I am concerned with is mostly instrumental. Most of the beliefs and practices that managers, in spite of the evidence, cling to, are intended to produce some external effect, rather than to release emotional impulses. But religious activities exist as well.

On the whole I have tried, objectively and dispassionately, to describe the management culture in the way that an anthropologist might describe a culture he has investigated, though with the relaxation of academic rigour one would expect in a book designed for a lay reader. Like any such anthropologist, my immediate experience has been limited to one particular branch of the culture. My field-work has been restricted to the family of tribes known as the publishing industry.

However, I have travelled among other peoples, and have cross-matched my experiences with those of other observers, both by talking with them and reading their reports. Nothing I have found has led me to lessen my belief that the patterns of behaviour in my own sub-culture are paralleled in every other.

By way of introduction I have little else to say. But to avoid McGregor's disillusion I should like to point out that I am not advocating any attempt to root out all magical and religious behaviour from management. To do so would be to disorient the entire culture and invite disaster.

Moreover it would be impossible. For the manager, like the primitive tribesman, lives in a world of insecurity and fear, peopled with ill-understood forces. It is a world in which he is intensely vulnerable. And like the primitive tribesman the manager is a human being. He will need to invent myths, to establish creeds, to cling to rituals, in the universal attempt to avoid the dark inhumanity of randomness and chance.

To disturb that is dangerous. To understand it is essential. For if we wish to understand the people we deal with, to influence them and control them – to *manage* – then the worst mistake we can make is to assume that the manager, even in the twentieth century, is a rational being.

1. Magic at Large

Once upon a time man lived at the mercy of an environment he could not understand. He hunted game – sometimes he found it, and sometimes he went hungry. He planted crops – sometimes they prospered and sometimes they failed. He sought out roots, berries, insects – sometimes they were plentiful, sometimes scarce. He fell ill – sometimes he recovered, sometimes he died. And in each case the reasons for success and failure were beyond his comprehension.

He lacked that understanding of the physical world on which our present culture prides itself. Whether in his way of life we see nobility or simply squalor, we are quite safe in pronouncing primitive man to be ignorant.

Of course he wouldn't feel that way. Or, if he did, he wouldn't admit it. And since the last person we ever admit anything to is ourselves, in his own mind he was perfectly happy that he knew all the answers. Occasionally he might want to consult his local wise man. Sometimes he might even travel to the next village, or even farther, to look for help. But in general he was secure in his conviction that the body of knowledge available to him was sufficient to account for everything that happened.

Thus the Pueblo Indians of New Mexico had no difficulty in accounting for a lack of rain – someone must have made a mistake in performing the complex rituals of the rain dances. Thinking back, it wouldn't be too difficult to point a finger at the particular performer and the particular mistake. Similarly the Dobuan islander, confronted with the failure of his yam crop, knew what had happened – someone had bewitched his plants and his own counter-charms hadn't been strong enough to protect them.

In our terms, of course, primitive man was kidding himself. His need for psychological security drove him to create a set of beliefs that enabled him to account for his environment and the events that took place in it. It led to the evolution of a system of rituals that enabled him to cause and control those events.

Today we are past all that. We are several centuries into the age of reason. Science and technology present us with either the actuality or the promise of control over our environment. Perhaps we cannot yet stop a thunderstorm or control a flood. But we know why they happen and we can mitigate the disasters they cause. We cannot summon up rain, but at least on occasion we can create rain by the satisfactorily mechanistic method of dropping ice into a cloud. And with modern irrigation we can lessen our dependence on the random benevolence of Nature.

In many other ways we are undeniably better equipped than our predecessor cultures. We can cure more illnesses, prevent more diseases, build stronger houses, produce food more abundantly and move ourselves and our goods more readily.

But to achieve that degree of mastery we have had to pay a price. Earlier cultures had only to contend with the simple and, to our eyes, impersonal forces of Nature. Onto that basic environment we have had to superimpose a man-made superstructure of social, economic and political forces that bring new and equally incomprehensible threats. In inventing money, we have invented inflation. In inventing world-wide trade we have invented the balance of payments and the slump. In the train of ever more potent technology we discover a multitude of intractable problems that we lump together and glibly label 'pollution'. All of these are as little understood as the thunder and floods and plagues of the primitive world. Like the primitive tribesman we cling to the belief that someone, somewhere, knows the answers. We need to know that, and so we know it.

Many of the old threats still remain outside our control. Cancer and heart disease evoke the same fascination and shadowy fears as the Black Death and leprosy a thousand years ago. And at perhaps the most basic level of all we have made no progress at all. We are still afraid of old age, of unattractiveness and social isolation, and of sexual inadequacy.

And where we have conquered the old fears, we have created new ones to take their place.

Contemporary Western civilization is as beset by insecurity as any earlier culture. It is hardly surprising that our reactions follow the behavioural patterns that have distinguished all human societies. We search for incantations, potions and spells to survive in the face of the threats we sense around us. We seek verbal and behavioural rituals that release some of our insecurity in the expression of solidarity.

Perhaps the most obvious example is in the attempt to achieve and retain sexual attractiveness, and the related search for ways to remain young. In our quest for potions and elixirs our culture is indistinguishable from its predecessors. Of course we have the advertising industry and the mass media to help us in our search. And we like to see the reassuring label 'scientific' tagged on to anything we buy. Instances are so multitudinous it may be superfluous to quote them, but one particular marketing leaflet I came across in a health food store is such a perfect illustration I cannot ignore it. Designed to promote a particular brand ('Barbara Cartland's Choice') of honey, its title is overtly 'The Magic of Honey', which also happens to be the title of a book by Miss Cartland, a popular romantic novelist and also President of the National Association for Health. In that capacity she has written the text of the leaflet, although, as she says, 'I am entirely impartial and have no financial interest in any way with the products recommended.'

The simplest way of showing how the magical appeal implicit in the title is juxtaposed with scientific arguments is to quote. 'There is nothing that gives you strength quicker and better than honey, as athletes have found since the beginning of time ... *Used in pharmacy for its beneficial demulcent properties ... Contains fruit sugar in ample quantities and is a speedy source of energy. The natives* [Maori] *use the honey for chest complaints* ... A woman wants to be loved and made a fuss of until she dies, and she can keep her husband loving her if she gives him Honey ... *Renowned for its astringent properties. Therefore much used as a haemostat. Trace elements found include larger amounts than normal of the B complex vitamins* ... Honey possesses some magical quality which can help us to feel young, so that old age is never troublesome. It doesn't matter being old in years, and I do believe that Honey, if taken every day, can help us to feel, look, and be young ... Another of the things Honey does is to strengthen the bladder *... a nervine – extract from the flowers is used as a carminative in stomach disorders* ... Honey was found in a tomb in Egypt which was known to be over 3,000 years old. It was in a perfect state of preservation and ready to eat.'

And so on. The italics are not mine. I have nothing against the leaflet. If it makes people happy and sells honey, that's fine. I certainly don't have enough biochemical or medical knowledge to pronounce on the validity of the claims. But my point is that neither do the people who buy the honey. They buy it on faith, as human beings have always bought love potions and youth elixirs. And the biochemical jargon serves exactly the same reassuring purpose as the mystic mumblings of witches and sorcerers.

The struggle for sexual attractiveness and youth, while it occupies so much of our time, is generally considered unworthy of serious attention. It won't worry anyone that our behaviour in this field is supernaturally motivated. It will perhaps be taken more seriously in connection with 'real' illnesses, infectious diseases and cancers for instance. The lay public's attitude to the more feared illnesses is probably as magical as it ever was, even though 'our' knowledge of the biological mechanisms underlying them is soundly based on empirical research. But in this case the public is protected from itself. In most developed countries at least, the law prevents the making of unjustified claims for medicines or treatments aimed at curing illness. Somehow this must involve the making of a subtly legalistic distinction between illness and ageing, between curing skin diseases, and 'keeping that youthful complexion'. I don't know precisely where the distinction lies, but it at least parallels the moralistic judgement that cosmetics are frivolous and medicines serious. By implication it recognizes that the lay attitude, unless restrained, will be the same to both.

A further field in which our behaviour is largely dominated by ritual of various kinds is the education and bringing up of children. Here the transience of fads and fashions is well recorded. So is the emotional dedication of their followers. I only really want to point out two things. From my point of view it is irrelevant whether the particular preacher concerned is himself a scientific research-worker, a sincere though non-empirical believer, or a charlatan – what counts is the attitude of his followers. Secondly, rituals in this field demonstrate a compound of instrumental and expressive motivations. The mother following the latest fashions in bringing up her children, and the education authority installing a system of 'comprehensive' education, are both acting in the sincere belief that they are doing something beneficial to the children (or 'society'). This is instrumental. But both are also behaving in a way that expresses their solidarity with the particular group to which they belong. This is expressive.

Marketing men have fastened on the need for the ritual expression of community as much as on the need for instrumental magic. Exploitation of this need is behind, for instance, the Heinz jingle that starts 'a million housewives every day ...' The jingle says nothing for the nutritive or other merits of baked beans. But it does reassure the housewife that in serving them she is expressing her membership of a vast community. Whether or not the beans actually do any good is, quite correctly, recognized as irrelevant by the advertiser.

A contrasting need to assert individuality also demands ritual expression. For some individuals this particular need may be dominant. In others the need to submerge in the safety of the crowd may be all that matters. Most of us need to do both. This paradoxical situation creates problems (in particular the see-sawing political tension between collectivist-centralized and liberal-anarchic movements). But they are soluble.

Again the marketing departments have helped find solutions. For instance, part of the success of the Ford Capri has undoubtedly been due to the wisdom of the company in making available a vast range of slightly differing versions. They emphasized the 'custom-built' aspects of the car in their advertising. The customer can simultaneously satisfy his need for community in belonging to the fellowship of Ford owners and his need for individual recognition by choosing his 'personalized' Capri.

An inverted example is visible in the story of Jensen Motors. As an out-and-out individualist's car, the Jensen languished. It found a steady but small stream of buyers. It didn't move to the profitable point until astute marketing by Carl Duerr, the turnaround man brought in to restore the company, established possession of the Jensen as a badge of membership in an esteemed caste.

In our society material possessions are almost the only 'identifiers' of this kind. The individual mainly asserts his identity by what he buys. In smaller and less mechanized cultures, individuality was more or less assured by the distinctions between occupations. The increasing erosion of individual and meaningful job activity has necessitated the establishment of surrogate means of expression. So we have the apparent paradox that women at a party must all be dressed in the same fashion, but must wear different dresses. Houses must conform to standard norms, but be painted and decorated differently. Holidays must be taken in an accepted range of resorts, but the choice of specific place must be different from that of one's everyday associates.

One almost expects irrational behaviour in consumers buying mass-produced goods, laymen faced by disease, mothers bringing up children, the middle-aged seeking youth. Yet the same magical and ritual attitudes are obvious in our handling of the major problems of economics and politics.

Judged by any government's record of achievement it is patently obvious that no one understands the way the economy works, not even in the limited way that chemists 'understand' the way that molecular bonding works. In Britain none of the economic measures introduced by successive governments have achieved their intended aims. Where they have roughly succeeded they have always been accompanied by unexpected and usually undesirable side effects that tended to negate the useful aspects. But even in more successful countries there has been no evidence that the successes were the direct result of deliberate and premeditated action.

The Western democracies have all used variants of the same

economic techniques. Superficially, they have 'worked' in some places and not in others. But anyone applying the experimental standards of science and technology to the processes of economic control would soon have decided that the correlation between measures and effects was low. He would have discovered that the theories on which the controls were based should be discarded as invalid. Discarding the verbiage, the logic and the rationalizations, he might well have focused on one fact. The only discernible distinction between the 'successful' countries and the 'unsuccessful' was in the extent to which their working populations expected a rising standard of living without changing their job activities.

There is a continuing attempt to make the facts fit theories that are only held because of their logical persuasiveness. As I will be pointing out throughout this book, logic is no criterion of empiricism. It is sometimes even its greatest enemy. The use of logical rationalization to explain away discrepancies between prediction and actuality is one of the major tools of the magician. But it is the major occupation of most economists and economic commentators.

At times we have seen an even more primitive thought-process at work – the invention of malevolent spirits to explain undesired effects. The most celebrated of such occasions was the invention by George Brown in 1964 of the 'gnomes of Zurich' to explain the deteriorating state of the British economy. As an economic theory it is on a par with the agricultural theory that cows run dry because the little people have been milking them. But like all the other accounts of mystical 'speculators' and capitalist 'conspirators', it gained a great deal of popular support. There is no visible evidence for their existence (or at least for their possession of extraordinary powers). Nor is there any visible evidence that the international banking community understands how to control economic processes any more effectively than national governments do.

But for most people it is preferable to hold such beliefs than to face up to the possible truth that no one really understands what they are doing. It is better to believe that supernatural forces are at work. It is better to conjure up a legendary hero like Lord Keynes and re-interpret his oracles, better to perform the traditional rituals of freeze and squeeze. It is easier to postulate an unending battle between the forces of good and evil than to accept that the forces of economics are uncomprehended (if not incomprehensible) and uncontrolled (if not uncontrollable).

In the same way the savage at the mercy of the elements must believe they are controlled by forces that can at least be placated. He must have faith that among the wise men of his tribe some at least understand the true nature of those forces and how to deal with them.

In *1984*, George Orwell supposes that the ultimate in degradation is loss of the 'freedom to say two plus two equals four'. I take him to mean the freedom to recognize 'self-evident' truths and express them. What he fears is the power of totalitarian government to influence not only beliefs that people outwardly hold, but even the truths that they themselves inwardly perceive. But he starts from an optimistic standpoint. For most people that freedom is already lost, not under the pressure of external authority, but by the structure of human nature itself. Free though we may in theory be to recognize objective facts, it is a freedom we rarely exercise. The facts we observe are the ones we expect and desire to see. And in almost everything we do our expectations and desires are formed by the same motivations that led our ancestors to invent magic and religion.

It is hardly surprising that the magico-religious attitude permeates our behaviour in the activity on which our material prosperity most depends – in industry and in commerce. In this area we are most proud of our objectivity and hard-headedness. Yet even here we invent supernatural forces, invent rituals, observe taboos and recite incantations. Of course we do not do so openly. This is not the language we use to describe our activities, and it is not the framework in which we normally view them.

The rest of this book is intended to show that in the process of management and the behaviour of managers we can see recreated the behaviour of our 'superstitious' ancestors.

2. The Worshippers

The time is around 9.30 in the morning, somewhere in England in the late sixties. A hundred or so business executives, sober-suited, sports-jacketed, with an occasional flowered tie, but no flared trousers, are almost filling the slightly faded Edwardian banqueting hall of an out-of-season hotel.

On the dais, the chairman has just sat down, resigned now to the early morning reception that greets early morning jokes. The man he has just introduced rises to his feet, rather too obviously laying down his pipe. A wisp of applause dies to an expectant, perhaps apprehensive, hush. The man has a considerable reputation as a successful manager, marketing director (in fact Marketing Director) of a company that is regularly in the *Times* top ten for profitability.

Living up to his reputation, he brooks no nonsense, adds no frills. A murmured thank you to the chair, then: 'Let us never forget that we are all of us in business for one thing only. To make a profit.'

The hush breaks, the apprehension goes. Audibly, feet slide forward and chairs ease back. Orthodoxy has been established. The incantation has been spoken. No one is going to be forced to query the framework of his world, to face the terrible question, 'Why?' Everyone can relax back into the comfortable communion of like minds, secure in his identity with his fellows, reassured by the rightness of his beliefs. Perhaps, scattered around, there are a few who have the honesty to feel guilty. They may realize that it is a long time since any of their actions was motivated by making a profit. But even their guilt heightens their identity. By the end of the conference they will leave with a sense of expiation, with a determination that in the future they will lead a better life.

Officially, we are watching 'a conference designed to give senior executives and directors a broader understanding of the central importance of the marketing function'. In fact it is a prayer meeting.

Prayer, unfortunately, is a word with many meanings. Originally 'to pray' is to ask for something. Most prayers are, in form at least, requests for something to happen. But not always. There are religions – Jainism and Buddhism, for example – which deny the existence of potent gods; but they still have prayer.

Even the Christian in congregation, murmuring the never-forgotten words of the Lord's Prayer, is highly unlikely to expect the prayer to be answered. He expects to continue to face (and fall for) temptations, just as he expects to continue to work for his daily bread. If he is sophisticated enough he will probably hold that it is in any case 'wrong' to pray for material help. Still he prays. For the act is not instrumental, though it is cast in that form, but expressive. It provides an opportunity to reaffirm one's faith, one's sense of order and rightness, one's place in society, one's *communion* with the group.

Which is what makes that Edwardian banqueting room a place of worship, the speaker a preacher, and the audience a congregation.

For the fact of the matter is that almost no one in business, judged by what he actually does, is in there to make a profit. For security, yes. For fellowship, yes. For status and self-esteem and power and comfort, yes. But the number of people in the audience I described whose behaviour is conditioned by the desire to make a profit is probably about equal to the number of people in a Victorian congregation (when Christianity was fashionable) whose behaviour was materially affected by Christ's commandments. If all the people who ritually subscribe to the belief that companies exist and people work for them to make a profit were really trying to do so, companies would make a vast amount more money than they do.

Of course, some people do try, just as there were and are christian Christians. But I could have made my speaker a member of a more extreme sect. I could have made him say that the purpose of business was to maximize profit (or return on investment or something) and it would have been just as believable. For some people it is an equally acceptable incantation. Yet it is even more vulnerable to any rational analysis. Herbert Simon years ago exploded any such belief quite as effectively as Darwin dealt with Christian Fundamentalism. Both creeds, however, have soundly established their ability to overcome any amount of factual evidence to the contrary.

As another of George Vetter's students put it: 'Faith is the power that enables us to believe things we know to be untrue.' Faith is an ineradicable trait of humanity in general and managers in particular. So, although nobody sane ever attempts to maximize – or optimize, it makes no difference – anything, a lot of people go around believing that they do. Or at the least believing that they should.

There are of course people who believe that to seek profit is wrong. They are members of a different culture altogether. The difference between them and management is a clash of religious belief that is outside the scope of this book, just as the 'rightness' or 'wrongness' of sexual intercourse was outside the scope of the Kinsey report.

If then we are faced with a manifestation of a religious impulse, if the marketing conference is a prayer meeting, if the obeisance to profit is a ritual incantation, what is the congregation worshipping? If they have a religion, what are its creeds, its dogmas, its rituals? How are its precepts enforced? And if it has gods, how and by whom are they served?

These questions will be answered in the rest of this book. But in order to establish a framework I must make some general points.

In the first place it is probably safer to say that we are faced with a magico-religious system, rather than simply a religion. It has both instrumental and expressive elements. Useless rituals are performed daily in the belief that they can 'produce results'. Even management conferences are believed by some people to be useful, and Training Boards encourage people to go to them. The religious and magical elements are in fact so closely intermingled that it is frequently impossible to separate them.

Moreover, it is a rich and relatively sophisticated system. It has more in common with the magico-religious systems of settled and economically well-off communities than with bare-existence cultures like that of the Australian aborigines. (However, there are relics of an earlier and more primitive time.)

Thus it is a learned system. The theology is complex. The theologians have compiled a vast and growing body of written lore. It is also a formal system. It has a formal priesthood (discussed in the next chapter), formal office-holders and a formal division of function.

But it is not monolithic. While a standard of orthodoxy can be traced out, there are a multitude of sects, some well-established and some new, of varying degrees of heresy. Once one starts to look at the finer details of ritual and belief each tribe in the culture may be discovered to have its own system. Even within the tribe clashing sects may exist.

It is, too, an established religion. Public observance counts for more than inner belief or private practice. However it is strong. To infringe publicly its tenets, or even to express openly some of the more reprehensible heresies, can lead to severe social punishment, including ostracism, excommunication and expulsion.

But exactly what is this magico-religious system of management?

Every magico-religious system postulates the existence of supernatural forces. Sometimes they are personified. By definition they are forces or beings possessing miraculous powers inaccessible to human beings, though they may be controlled or at least placated by certain rituals or incantations.

In the management system this place is mainly taken by the shareholder. Objectively, the average shareholder in the average company has about as much power to influence events as the demons of Indian mythology. Nevertheless they are believed to have such power. The belief is expressed not only verbally, but behaviourally. (An alternative way of expressing the same point is to say that managers behave as if shareholders had power, and rationalize the behaviour by expressing the belief. It comes to the same thing, but the second formulation will leave some psychologist friends of mine a lot happier.)

Such a belief can always be expressed in two ways, through

acts and prayers designed to induce the gods to exercise their power, and through rites and incantations to prevent or restrain them from doing so. In management, the latter is virtually universal. The essence of the taboo structure that I will be discussing later is largely to avoid acts that will arouse the shareholder to action. As in most magico-religious cultures, the aim of ceremonies like the Annual General Meeting is to keep the supernatural powers dormant, to avoid their attention, or, if they must be roused, to divert them to an insignificant or sacrificial object.

However, prayers for intercession are sometimes heard. They continue to be made even though the likelihood of any effective result is of the same order of magnitude as prayers to the deities of any other religion. The Christian bereft of any other resource will put his trust in God to deliver him from tyranny. The manager suffering from a misguided directorate that is leading his company to disaster will put his trust in 'the shareholders' to rescue the situation – especially that particular category of higher gods known as 'the institutions'.

A possible objection to the analogy is that the manager's gods 'actually' exist in a way that the gods of other cultures do not. Through possession of equity – the hallmark of divinity – the manager may indeed himself be a god. But the objection does not hold. It only arises from a particularly Judaeo-Christian way of looking at things. The gods of other cultures – the sun, the moon, the thunderstorm, the sea – are also visible and tangible. They exist, though they do not have the powers ascribed to them. They become abstract personifications. The 'shareholder' or 'the institution' that the manager deifies and seeks to placate is also an abstract personification.

This is even more true in those cases where the shareholder is a single owner. He is not only visible but familiar. The supernatural power is still ascribed, and to arouse his attention is still to court disaster. Familiarity does not breed contempt.

(At this point it may be necessary to remember that we are talking about the 'official' religion professed by the manager. He may or may not actually believe, but he acts and talks as though he does.)

*

A second major feature of the orthodox creed is the ascription of supernatural existence to the 'company'. Objectively and rationally speaking, the 'company' does not exist at all, except in so far as it is a heterogeneous collection of people. In order to facilitate the mutual ownership and use of assets, and for other technical reasons, the corporation is treated in law as a person. It is a legal fiction, but a fiction nonetheless. (Anyone too steeped in the official religion to accept this point readily would do well to read T. D. Weldon's account of the state in *The Vocabulary of Politics*, a 1951 Pelican Original which is unfortunately difficult to get hold of.)

However, by a process which owes its origin to Plato and much of its modern popularity to Hegel, the corporation is idealized. It is transmuted into a being in its own right, with, among other things, a 'purpose'. Now in any real sense, only a living being can have a purpose of its own. A company, like a hammer, can only have a purpose in so far as it is endowed with one by its creator or its user. But in most varieties of the basic religion it is considered essential, let alone possible, to talk of the company having a purpose with the implication that it has a will of its own.

In much the same way states, cities and institutions have throughout history been endowed with personae. Frequently, as in classical Rome, they have been formally worshipped. They have generally been seen as entities demanding loyalty and service, usually with disastrous consequences. In management the company is rarely worshipped in any full sense (though it sometimes gets very close, as in I B M with the adulation paid to both the company and the just-ending Watson dynasty). But it is almost invariably seen in a sacred light. Loyalty and dedication to it are essential elements of the creed.

Originally 'the company' signified the shareholders, as with 'the company of merchant adventurers trading into Hudson's Bay'. It would be moderately rational if it were still seen in the same light. However in most management preaching a subtle distinction is still made between the 'company' and the 'shareholders' that baffles the understanding. It is not even equated with 'shareholders and employees', which would still make empirical sense. With the sects that elevate this particular facet of the orthodox belief to the position of the central dogma, the cyberneticists, the distinctions drawn surpass those drawn in Trinitarian doctrine. One suspects they would make a Talmudist pause for thought.

Most of the world's religions enjoin a specific way of life on their members. As the Jew, the Muslim and the Christian are required to do God's bidding, and the Buddhist is exhorted to follow the Eightfold Path to Nirvana, so the manager is told to make profits.

Usually, as I pointed out earlier, he takes very little notice of the exhortation, no more in fact than the Jew, Muslim, Christian or Buddhist does. But the teaching is so ingrained that he feels guilty if his lapses are brought to his attention, and he would consider it the height of impropriety to suggest that the exhortation has anything less than the status of a revealed truth. It is an interesting and illuminating experiment to ask a normal believer in the management creed simply to say, for instance: 'The purpose of business is to give people something to do.' He will prevaricate, argue, look uneasy, dismiss it as silly and perform all manner of expiatory rituals. Frequently he will simply refuse to say it – even if no one else is there to hear him. This is not rational behaviour. It is religious behaviour. Try asking a member of any other faith to commit an equivalent blasphemy. The reactions will be the same.

Not surprisingly, the repetition of incantations connected with the making of profit is a major feature of most of the expressive rituals of the system. Just as the central Christian prayer begins with 'Thy will be done'.

In summary form these three points cover the essentials of the orthodox religion. They are common to most schools, although especially in recent years many sects have arisen who are willing to challenge the deification of the shareholder. I will be discussing such heresies at various points throughout the book. It is worth pointing out now that they have only gained any kind of a following where they have elevated some other deity to the prime position. Most of them stick to the 'company', though an interesting and favourite newcomer is

the 'Market' – both in the sense of the customer and the personified Stock Exchange. But very few have dared to challenge
the sanctity of profit.

Over the remainder of this book the whole picture of a complex magico-religious sytem will become clearer. As a first step
I would like to turn my attention away from the creed itself
back to its protagonists. And in particular to those who are
dedicated specifically to serving its gods and ensuring that the
worshippers are reminded of, and kept to, the narrow paths of
virtue – to the priests of the religion.

3. The Priests

A little while ago, a psychologist friend of mine, Valerie Barden, gave a series of personality tests to 400 volunteers who were taking courses at Ashridge Management College. The results were illuminating in many ways, but especially in that one group of managers stood out as significantly different from the rest. The bulk of the managers tended to be more expedient and suspicious than the general population. They were 'unsteady and lacking in perseverance, sometimes impatient and obstructive ... mistrusting and doubtful'. The variant group on the other hand were more likely to be 'practical, realistic, independent ... but uncultured, sometimes phlegmatic, hard, cynical and smug'. They also tended to be more independent, resolute, accustomed to going their own way, making decisions and taking action on their own.

The variant group were the accountants.

If managers inhabit an insecure and chaotic world, which they can only cope with through ritual, incantation and clinging to magical and superstitious beliefs, one would expect them to exhibit the personality features revealed by the tests above. But why should accountants be different – be more self-assured, self-reliant, independent? In a word, smug? The answer of course is simple. They *know* they are right.

The average manager is still troubled by doubt and by uncertainty about the purpose of business. Therefore he still needs reassurance from the kind of prayer meeting I described in the last chapter. The accountant is past all that.

A lengthy, Jesuitical, educational programme, years of conditioning as an articled clerk before he is formally qualified, ensure that the accountant inhabits a world of which the moral framework is comfortingly rigid. He is the inheritor of the self-righteous certainty which has belonged to the Pharisee, the

Inquisitor, the Witch-hunter. He displays the hallmark of the member of an established priesthood.

For the moment, whether or not the accountants *are* right is immaterial. In formulating behaviour their conviction is what matters. It is enough to point out that their conviction is unshakeable by any amount of factual evidence that the audited books of a company can be totally misleading. It is magico-religious. If the basic tenets of the management creed are the deification of the 'shareholder', the deification of the 'company', and insistence on making profit as the 'right' way of life, then the prophets and priests of the creed are without doubt the members of the chartered accountancy institutions.

That isn't to say they do not have a useful function. Priesthoods usually do, just as religion does, buried though it may be under a welter of mumbo-jumbo and superstition. In Babylon and Egypt someone had to keep track of the seasons, to record the rise and fall of the rivers. In management someone has to keep track of trading performance, to record the rise and fall of cash flows. As Keeper of the Books – a traditional priestly title – the accountant has a rational and useful role. But the accountant who sticks to it is a rare fish. Certainly the officers of the established institutions would claim that it was a minor part of their usefulness. After all, it doesn't offer much in the way of power or esteem to an ambitious or intelligent man – and Valerie Barden's studies showed accountants on the whole as more intelligent than the average manager.

So the accountant, the specialist in recording what did happen, projects himself and is accepted as the prophet and the moral guide. He is the man who knows what will happen and what ought to happen. In those roles he has been anticipated by priesthoods throughout the ages.

Let's look for a while at some of the characteristics by which a priesthood can be identified.

It is worth noting that priesthoods don't exist in truly primitive societies like those of the North American Indians, the Australian aborigines and the African Bushmen. Such cultures may have highly developed religious and moral senses. The aboriginal pygmy inhabitants of the Philippines held to their rigorous monogamy in spite of the polygamous behaviour of the invading Malays. But they lack formal institutions. In particular they lack a formally qualified and specialized group of people responsible for the expression and protection of their religious beliefs. Fritz Kern, the German archaeologist and anthropologist, named such cultures 'wildbooters'. There are traces of similar cultures in management, and I will use the term in referring to them elsewhere in this book.

There is room for a priesthood only when the culture has been established, has settled, and is generating enough economic surplus to free at least some of its members from the necessity of directly productive labour. Moreover the culture must be literate – even though one can watch embryonic priesthoods forming in preliterate cultures like those of the East African Masai and Nandi. Possession of the common bond of literacy may well be the chief distinguishing attribute of the priests.

Now, except in the world of the small entrepreneur and the one-man-show, it is pretty obvious that management today is past the wildbooter stage. Its organization is complex and roles are well-differentiated. There is a considerable economic surplus available for the maintenance of non-productive members. The managerial culture has reached something like the level of ancient Egypt or Crete, or perhaps even classical Greece and Rome. One would expect it to be supporting some kind of priesthood.

'Some kind of' is an important qualification, because the number of different varieties and types of priesthood is considerable. But in spite of that there are certain attributes that are almost invariably present, and that accountancy must have if our identification is to be verified. Let's look at them in turn.

Perhaps the most obvious hallmark of a priesthood is that it is *organized*. Normally there is a hierarchy (the word means 'government by priests'). Even in cases where a strictly pyramidal hierarchy does not exist there are well-defined tasks and roles, and equally well-defined grades and divisions. In fact, disciplinary powers can be exerted only with an organization, and without disciplinary powers most of the other priestly attributes could not be maintained.

Invariably too priests are the possessors of *arcane knowledge* and skills denied, by and large, to the layman. The possession of this knowledge and skill provides the priest with his special powers to demand support from the community. Of course traditionally his knowledge is cosmological. The priest knows the secrets of nature, the ways and wishes of the gods and spirits. The skills are also mystical. The priest knows how to intercede with the supernatural, and in some cases even how to constrain and control it.

In the more primitive cultures the total body of such knowledge may be small. It multiplies as time goes by until in the well-developed communities it may well require vast libraries to house it, and no one priest will be expected to know it all.

But the body of knowledge tends to grow by the accumulation of commentaries and commentaries on commentaries. More and more is written about less and less. The content of the original kernel of knowledge hardly changes. Indeed change will normally be passionately resisted. As a result the priestly knowledge will become outdated, and the services of the priesthood be required less and less by the community. This can happen through the supplanting of priestly knowledge by science and technology, as in our own culture. It can happen also by the substitution of more exotic forms of magic and religion, as happened in the later Roman Empire. On occasion both processes may take place simultaneously. They did in the Hellenistic culture that flourished in the Eastern Mediterranean between the reign of Alexander and the advent of Christianity.

Membership in a priesthood is jealously guarded. It is open only to a special segment of the population. The more primitive the society, the more likely the qualification is to be hereditary. The embryonic priests of the Masai and Nandi whom I mentioned earlier – the *laibons* and the *orkoiyots* – were of necessity members of a certain lineage. However, the hereditary qualification is still dominant in the oldest of the major current religions, Judaism and Hinduism.

Other than birth, the two most common qualifications are ability and vocation. In theory the ability requirement is simply a high enough level of intellectual and physical capacity to understand and exercise the relevant body of knowledge and skills. In many cultures, however, it has been used to guarantee that priests had a higher level of attainment than the rest of the population. (Where chastity is enjoined on the priesthood, this can of course have unfortunate genetic consequences.)

Vocation I am using in its original sense of 'being called'. The priest must have been 'chosen' by whatever supernatural powers are believed to exist. In the Christian churches evidence of vocation is normally required, though proof rarely needs to be as rigorous as it is among the Barundi of Tanzania, where, apart from inheritance, the only ways of being accepted as a *kiranga* are to be struck by lightning or to go into a trance during a religious ceremony.

An *initiation* ritual is an invariable accompaniment of a candidate's entry into the priesthood. Normally it includes an extensive period of novitiate to test competence and dedication. Thus among the Sabians of Iraq, the rituals of initiation start from birth, for the future priest must be physically without flaw. He must follow a course of study which may last anything from nine to seventeen years. At one stage he must pass seven days and nights confined in a hut without excreting or sleeping. He must spend sixty days without any emission of seminal fluid. And on top of that he must be voted for by an assembly of the people, and be the legitimate son of a priest to start with.

Few cultures are that rigorous, but the essential elements are common. The candidate must demonstrate his purity. He must acquire the sacred knowledge; and he must demonstrate his ability to conform to certain disciplines.

The priesthoods enforce strict *discipline* on their members. Priests are expected to conform to stricter codes of behaviour than laymen. The criteria of virtue may be identical for the layman and the priest, but the priest will be expected to achieve higher standards. Thus in a culture where chastity is considered a virtue, the priest may be required to be totally celibate, while the layman will be subjected to only a limited amount of regulation.

A minor aspect of the discipline which a priest is expected to observe concerns dress. Priests will be expected to dress distinctively. (Include physical mutilation and tattooing as dress, forgetting for the moment any ritual significance in the scarification as such.) In cultures where fashions in dress change, the priestly dress tends to reflect outdated fashion. This is an aspect of the conservation which is part of the next attribute for discussion.

Guardianship is an essential role of any priesthood. The priest will always see himself as the maintainer of public morality. This function distinguishes him from the sorcerers who are the subject of the next chapter. As the preserver of moral standards he is likely to be biased in favour of conservatism on all fronts. While there may be radical-minded priests, the institution as a whole is likely to throw its weight on to the side of preserving the *status quo* of the culture, and to exercise disciplinary powers over any members who work against it. Effectively, any challenge to the established order of society is a challenge to the position of the established church within it.

(This may not be true of the priesthood of a new religion, which may well advocate radical social change as part of its attempt to win a position for itself, or to enforce the observance of a new morality. However, the more it wins acceptance, the more it turns to conservatism. Thus where Communism is firmly entrenched the advocacy of change is firmly repressed. On the other hand, where Christianity has lost its established footing, as in Protestant Western Europe, the Church has displayed its willingness to experiment – even lead – movements of social protest. New cults however are not properly the subject of this chapter: they belong rather to later ones.)

Finally, *mediation* represents probably the central role of any priesthood. Because of his special relationship with the gods the kernel of the priest's activities becomes the task of mediating between man and the divine. In some cultures this role is restricted to supplication. Elsewhere the priest is assumed actually to be able to constrain the deity.

From his special relationship with the gods the priest derives his authority and power in the community. It evinces itself in his power to predict and control the course of nature. As belief in that power wanes, his authority diminishes.

It is worth noting however that simple failure on the priest's part is rarely enough to shake the beliefs of his congregation. Faith, as I have pointed out, is not subject to factual disproof. Failure can always be rationalized, and the need for expression normally conquers the demands of instrumentality. Thus faith is only diminished by the substitution of alternative faiths. Religion and magic are only weakened by new systems which offer superior methods of achieving results, and a more satisfactory release for the perennial human needs of expression.

We have seven attributes to identify an institution which is playing the role of a priesthood in its culture. Let us see how accountancy measures up to the pattern.

Self-evidently accountancy is an *organized* profession. While there may be more than one school, each is formally instituted and is governed by a specific authority. The hierarchy is loose, but roles are well-differentiated and defined. Thus, to take parallels from the Christian church, we have:

the lay priest: the accountant working for a company;
the mendicant priest: the professional accountant in a partnership;
the monastic priest: the banker, who, while not strictly an accountant, serves much the same ends in a separate and semi-isolated unit;
the father confessor: the auditing accountant to whom everything is (officially) revealed, and who then grants absolution.

We also have the equivalent of the priest-king in non-Christian cultures: the accountant/chief executive.

Possession of *arcane knowledge* is again an obvious characteristic of the accountancy profession. Its specific knowledge and skills could be compressed into one textbook and taught as part of an O-level mathematics course. The resemblance to the arcane knowledge of other priesthoods is obvious, as is the fact that there has been no significant change in the basic tenets since the profession was established. Refinement has been piled on refinement. The esoteric meanings of the balance sheet and the profit and loss account remain the same, just as the volumes of exegesis of the Talmud or the thousands of books of theological disputation produced by the Christian churches have left untouched the foundations laid down by the originators of the system. They must do so. The original revelation is beyond challenge.

In spite of its essential simplicity, the vast majority of managers are convinced of their own inability to acquire such knowledge. They are innumerate in the same way that the lay masses of the Bronze and early Iron Age cultures were illiterate. Granted there are increasing numbers of heretics around who are willing to challenge this accepted authority. There are even anti-priests. But heresy is a common enough phenomenon at least in developed societies, and it can only arise where there is already an entrenched priesthood.

Membership of the profession is as regulated as membership of any priesthood in times past or present. As one would expect in a developed culture, the profession is restricted to a selective elite, not a hereditary one. However, unless he is exceptionally unsuitable on some other ground, the son of an accountant is ensured of acceptance, as normally is any other close relative. Belief in the hereditary transmission of the particular qualities that mark a man out as suitable for the office is widespread.

Those qualities are of two kinds. The candidate for membership must be intellectually equipped to assimilate the esoteric knowledge of the cult. He must also be morally pure, in that he must have an unblemished record of honesty in money matters, and be – by the normal standards of the management culture – abnormally chaste and sober. Total abstinence is not insisted upon, though it may prove advantageous in obtaining advancement.

Dishonest and immoral accountants undoubtedly exist, just as supposedly celibate priests have been known to prove unchaste. All that matters for our purpose is that the accountancy profession is regarded as a morally superior elite.

The *initiation* procedure required of a candidate for admission to the profession is predictably complex and lengthy. On the assumption that the knowledge possessed by the accountant is valid and useful, it would be rational for the initiation procedure to require evidence of its attainment. A test of such knowledge does indeed form part of the requirement. But on its own it is insufficient. It must be acquired by spending a ritual length of time as a novice serving ordained accountants and performing menial tasks.

Such practices become less and less suited to the demands of industry, and sporadic attempts are made to change them. But the profession resists any such attacks on its purity. No amount of financial expertise or even genius is accepted as valid unless it is acquired in the ritualistically correct manner.

Even minor changes are strenuously resisted. Thus until recently the novice was required to serve, not only under an ordained member, but specifically in a mendicant house. This has cracked somewhat. Some of the institutions now allow training in industry. Others still hold out. In October 1970 the president of the Scottish Institute of Chartered Accountants reported his council's decision that 'proposals to train in industry by the Scottish Institute on its own should not be put to members at the present time, and that we should continue for the present to train only in practising offices'. Instead, the Institute was preparing a 'diploma in accounting' which 'could be useful to offices or companies wishing to recruit staff for accounting functions which did not require the whole range of skills of its members'.

Objectively such intransigence is hard to account for. No diploma course worth attending could be a lesser challenge intellectually than the present accountancy examinations. But seeing the profession as a priesthood, the importance of serving the novitiate becomes clear. It is not that the man with the diploma will lack any significant knowledge or skill. But he will not have been purified, and he will not have been properly conditioned. He will not have demonstrated his vocation and will not have achieved the right level of sanctity. Therefore he cannot command the mystical powers of the accountant, no matter how great his practical abilities.

That accountants are more *disciplined* than their colleagues can hardly be disputed. Indeed the institutions pride themselves on the fact. They enforce stricter standards of financial honesty and have requirements of chastity and sobriety. Among managers in general, standards of behaviour in these two areas are rather complicated, as will become apparent in the later chapters on taboos, but the accountant is expected to observe more stringent rules. Similarly, flamboyant behaviour and egregious consumption are generally considered wrong for managers, but the strictures fall more heavily on the accountant who offends. While in the higher grades the accountant will be expected to live well by the normal standards of culture, he will be expected to consume less than laymen of similar standing. Such restrictions extend to the way of dressing, though there is no priestly uniform. Unsuitable styles would automatically lead to rejection as a candidate for the novitiate. Even at a later stage, after ordination, it could well lead to his vocation being withdrawn, though it would not lead to ritual defrocking.

As I pointed out, one would expect the definition of virtue to be the same among laymen as among members of the profession, but the expectation of attainment to be greater. The sense of shock on seeing an accountant behave improperly is much greater than on seeing a lay manager do so. It is a highly significant factor in identifying the accountant as a priest.

Guardianship is certainly one role of the accountant. There is a widely accepted proverb: 'The accountant's job is to protect the company against the manager.' The accountant may act as censor. He may also be the executioner. 'Having the accountants in' is enough to lay a slight chill on the heart of any averagely sinful manager. The reserve with which accountants are normally treated by managers parallels what must have been the reaction of any lay member of sixteenth-century Spanish society to social contact with a Jesuit.

But if he is both censor and executioner, the accountant is also confessor and giver of absolution. Each community in the culture is required annually to have its conduct investigated by a specially designated order of accountants, and to seek ritual absolution. The absolution may have various forms. A common formula is:

'In our opinion the group balance sheet and group profit and loss account comply with the Companies Acts of 1948 and 1967, and respectively give a fair and true view of the state of affairs at 28 February 1970, and of the profit for the year ended on that date.'

Longer-winded than '*Ego te absolvo*', the message is much the same. As in Catholicism, the words are often pronounced over an unredeemed sinner. But in both cases, the existence of unrevealed sins is not held to reflect on the competence of the confessor, and will negate the absolution. Neither pronouncement is therefore of any great objective validity. Though I wish my Latin were good enough to translate:

'To the best of my knowledge and belief, and on the basis of the information with which I have been provided, in my opinion the record of your conduct complies with the Commandments of 1000 B.C. and A.D. 30–33, and gives a true and fair view of the state of affairs of your soul at this date, and of your conduct during the year now ended.

That leaves *mediation* as an outstanding attribute. As we have seen in the last chapter usually the divine figure in the system is the shareholder, supplemented by the giving of mystic status to the company itself. If accountancy is a priesthood it must have a central role in the process of mediation between the human and the divine. The accountant does play precisely this role.

Managers increasingly complain that the activities of accountants are irrelevant to their task of managing the business. But it is only a misunderstanding of the important mediatory role that makes those managers think that accountants *should* be helping them manage. For the activities of accountants are centred around the annual (or seasonal) rites of the Balance Sheet and the Profit and Loss Account. The sole purpose of these rites is mediatory.

They exist simply to placate the shareholders, their watchdogs the Press, and other luminaries of the pantheon like stockbrokers and investment analysts.

In his confessor role, the auditor/accountant is also playing a mediatory part. It might be possible to argue, however, that his activities are as important in satisfying the expressive need of the manager for absolution as they are in pursuing his instrumental requirement for placating the supernatural.

Moreover, the accountant will usually be looked upon by his lay associates as a special source of information about, and influence upon, that particular segment of the supernatural world, the stock market. Objectively there is no reason why they should. Accountancy training isn't particularly relevant to estimating the course of the market, accountants are not noticeably great speculators, and on the whole merchant banks and other investment houses don't particularly rush to employ them. But in any boardroom decision involving the state of the market, the voice of the accountant is likely to be heard with *ex cathedra* respect.

On all seven counts, therefore, the accountancy profession matches the pattern we outlined for a priesthood. The identification helps to clarify such otherwise inexplicable factors as the insistence on a long and formal novitiate, and the practical uselessness of the Annual Report. Indeed it helps explain the very fact that the accountant is seen as something simultaneously more and less than a financial expert. Less, because he can freely admit to lack of 'special' knowledge without endangering his status. Similarly a priest can freely admit to not being 'up with' the latest psychological teaching without endangering his status as an adviser on behaviour. And more, because he is surrounded by a special halo of status as the initiate of a superior moral caste.

From a practical point of view the accountant is more likely to be a handicap than a help in the day-to-day management of his company, indeed to any realistic method of planning ahead. Since this truth is beginning to be more widely recognized in the more rational segments of industry, substitutes are beginning to be sought elsewhere. Unfortunately, to reject the priesthood is not to reject religion, and to reject the established religion is not to reject irrationality. The main effect of this development has therefore been the spawning of a number of alternative cults, themselves magico-religious in nature, and the seeking out of sorcerers whose spells will be more effective than the traditional wisdom.

Some of these I will be dealing with in the next chapter. In the meantime I should like to point out that the identification of the accountant's role as priestly, and as substantially irrelevant to the practical business of running the company, is not to advocate its abolition or suppression. The Catholic or the Jew requires the solace and comfort of the eternal framework of

their religion. Similarly the manager needs the reassurance of
the accountant's presence and blessing. He needs the sense of
expiation and well-being that follows a successful auditor's report.

Even if he has passed to other means of satisfying these
expressive needs, the individual freethinker cannot afford to
buck the system. After performing the necessary annual rites
he can only hope for one thing. It is to preserve his sense of
reality as well as Galileo, who on leaving the room where he
had ritually asserted his belief in the fixed and unchanging
position of the Earth at the centre of the universe, was heard
to mutter: *'Eppur se muove'* – 'It *does* move.'

4. The Sorcerers

While the priesthood is a phenomenon associated only with highly developed cultures, the priest's predecessor and major rival, the independent 'wise man', is a universal phenomenon. Sometimes he is called sorcerer, sometimes magician, shaman, wizard, witch (or witch-doctor), medicine man – to use only a handful of the variety of words in common English usage.

Before attempting to locate them in the management culture it is worth spending some time identifying the hallmarks by which they can be recognized. They are always people who are considered to be equipped with powers not available to ordinary men and women. The special power may be broad and extend to most if not all areas of human activity or it may be restricted to one particular gift. Typical of the first kind are the witches of medieval and early modern Europe and the sorcerers of most parts of Africa. An example of the second kind is provided by the magically endowed chiefs of Tikopia, each of whom had his own special role to play in performing the 'work of the gods'.

Broad or narrow, the major distinction is between those whose power is supernatural and those whose power results from systematically acquired knowledge. After the exposition by Evans-Pritchard of witchcraft among the Zande of the Sudan-Congo border it has become conventional to designate the first group as 'witches', though this is rather different from the traditional use of 'witch' in English. For the second group standard usage prescribes the word 'sorcerer'; the body of his occult knowledge is called his 'medicine' (again at the risk of a clash with colloquial English).

It isn't always easy to make the sharp distinction. Respect is often reserved to practitioners who can boast both qualifications. Nevertheless pure examples do exist. Among the Plains Indians of North America supernatural power could only be acquired as the result of a vision, and the vision alone was enough. As Ruth Benedict describes in *Patterns of Culture*, they were prepared to go to extraordinary lengths to achieve such a vision. '... they cut strips from the skin of their arms, they struck off fingers, they swung themselves from tall poles by straps inserted under the muscles of their shoulders. They went without food and water for extreme periods ... Sometimes they stood motionless, their hands tied behind them, or they staked out a tiny spot from which they could not move till they had received their blessing.'

In other cultures, the supernatural powers are straightforwardly inherited. In yet others they are associated with liability to specific diseases, typically epilepsy and catalepsy.

Examples in which supernatural power is acquired solely by learning are rarer, though of course the strong European tradition of the wizard, white-whiskered and buried among arcane books in his secret cell, does provide one example. The more literate the culture, the greater is the reliance placed on learning at the expense of mysticism. Since we have already identified the management culture as a relatively sophisticated and literate one, one would therefore expect its wise men to approximate the picture of the sorcerer rather than to resemble the born witch, whose powers are bestowed upon him unsought, or who acquires them, sometimes literally, in a lightning stroke.

The formal priesthood develops of course out of the institution of the wise man, but the priest never supersedes the independent practitioner. Even when an established religion is at its most powerful, as in Israel or medieval Europe, the priest and the sorcerer exist in competition and, occasionally, in collaboration. When religions decay and lose the allegiance of the culture, sorcerers, in one guise or another, flourish. New sects develop around them either as heretical variants of orthodoxy or as something totally different. In time, one such sect is likely to become powerful enough to establish itself as a received religion, bringing the cycle full circle.

Thus Christianity evolved from the kaleidoscope of sects that characterized the latter Roman Empire after the decay of the old gods. In Polynesia the confrontation between the native religions and the superior European powers led to the spread of the cargo cults. Much the same thing is happening in management now.

Not that the set of beliefs I described in Chapter 2 is in danger of being shaken. While the service paid to profit may be lip-service it remains firm, even in the U S where the attacks on the profit motive are largely confined to academics and intellectuals. In the U K the adoption of profit-worship in academic and government circles, even by the Labour Party, has left it more securely entrenched than ever.

But the hierarchy itself is under considerable attack, not so much for the principles it preaches, as for the failure of its rituals to achieve their end. Some of the most spectacular failures of recent years have happened despite rigorous regard for the rituals prescribed by the established hierarchy of accountants. In some of the more extreme cases – Rolls Razor, the motor insurance failures – it has been possible to claim, as a Christian might when faced with the failure of his prayers, that while the outward forms were respected, inner dedication was lacking. Or it has been possible to discover flaws in the performance of the rituals. Indeed, an essential part of magico-religious systems is the ability to justify failure by the *ex post facto* uncovering of error. The rain didn't come because a line was left out of a spell. The curative medicine failed because the frog was caught at the new moon and not at the full.

But some failures cannot all that easily be explained away. There is no evidence that the managers of General Dynamics or even Penn Central were in anything but a state of grace when their times of trouble came. Scrupulous attention to accountancy rituals did nothing to save A E I or I P C from decay and annexation. A large number of managers have seen the same thing happening in many smaller and less sensational ways and criticism of the orthodox priesthood is becoming more and more common. Most management conferences on either side of the Atlantic include some kind of attack on orthodox accountancy.

Managers seek recourse to unorthodox sources of power and knowledge. And since their culture is a semi-literate one, they seek help chiefly from sorcerers who have developed their own medicines to ensure salvation through profit. They call them consultants.

The Polynesian islander wishing to build a canoe will seek advice about the wood he should choose for maximum buoyancy, and in doing so he acts in a rational and empirically justifiable manner. But he will also act in a magical manner in seeking advice about charms or incantations he should use to make the canoe go faster. The first consultant we may safely call a technologist; the second – probably, in practice, the same man – we would unhesitatingly dismiss as a magician. To the Polynesian the distinction does not exist. As a matter of fact, it is rarely made in our own culture. Only a small part of the service which managers seek from consultants is un-compromisingly technological in nature.

The parallel between the primitive and the manager may emerge from a few descriptions of the primitive's attitude to his 'consultants'.

Ernest Crawley explains: 'Every individual, though doubtful of his own magic powers, has no doubt about the possible powers of any other person.' He mentions 'the common belief that danger attaches to the first of any fruits or meats' and says: 'A similar idea underlies the common diffidence about beginning an act or doing something for the first time.'

And Lucy Mair tells us: 'Any answer is likely to be unpopular with someone, but it is often possible to try another diviner or another method if you don't like the first one. A wholly unexpected answer is unknown.' She goes on to say about the primitives: 'They may be sceptical about the genuineness of particular practitioners, but everyone believes there are genuine ones somewhere; in time of real trouble they could have no hope without this belief.'

Finally, here is a quotation from Raymond Firth's *Rank and Religion in Tikopia*: 'Though often spoken of collectively, spirit mediums practised separately. They were not an organized body: they did not consult [each other] on cases, and apparently did not discuss "business" among themselves. If one medium failed to effect a cure the patient was carried to another. Payment was apt to be by results: only a medium in

whose care a patient recovered, or who seemed to have benefited, usually received recompense.'

The quotations refer to members of primitive cultures. With
the possible exception of the last part of the quotation from
Firth all of them could well have been written about managers
and consultants. (The difference in billing arrangements says
more for the willingness of sorcerers to accept empirical tests
than it militates against the identification of modern consultants with their primitive forebears.)

Most managers, aware of their own inadequacy in dealing
with the more esoteric topics of management theory, are as
ready as the primitive tribesman to ascribe superior power to
strangers – privately if not publicly. Most bosses will assume
that outside specialists command more powerful medicine than
their own subordinates, for no other reason than that they are
from outside. The mechanism is best seen in action when a
consultant is invited to join a company full-time. It is rarely
more than six months before his new superiors are again feeling a nagging need for 'outside' advice. Their vague and ill-
defined sense of something missing is an infallible indicator
that a magico-religious principle is involved.

Equally it is true that consultancy is felt to be most necessary when something is being done for the first time. And if
the first consultant comes up with suggestions that aren't liked,
often on avowedly emotional grounds, another will be commissioned. In both cases, as Miss Mair says, the answers are
hardly unexpected. Indeed in our society the kind of answer
required, rather than the kind of problem, tends to dictate the
choice of consultant in the first place. If one wants a McKinsey solution, a Booz Allen solution or an Urwick Orr solution,
then one goes to McKinsey, Booz Allen or Urwick Orr. The
answer will be predictable, and the consultancy probably, from
an objective point of view, unnecessary. But the prescribed
solution will have the blessing and mystic force of the right
name.

Miss Mair's second quotation holds just as strongly. An
hour or so in any reasonably well-patronized restaurant or
bar close to a company where consultants are currently 'in'
will produce a notebook full of evidence that managers are

frequently 'sceptical about the genuineness of particular practitioners', notably those they have met in the flesh. But no matter how bitter their recriminations against specific individuals the most sceptical managers will invariably admit that genuinely useful consultants do exist. Somewhere. Like the primitive they need to think so. So they do.

So far the argument may appear rather sketchy. But before clinching it we will find it worthwhile to spend some time looking at different types of consultant and the roles they play in business. There are parallels with the various types of sorcerer and the roles they play in primitive society which are illuminating.

I have already referred to the difference between the witch and the sorcerer. On the basis of this definition witches in management are rare. Occasionally a figure like Herzberg or McGregor (as I pointed out in the Introduction) is hailed in a manner that indicates he is being viewed as a witch rather than a sorcerer. A recent rather sickening B B C documentary on the work of Hermann Kahn – the thinker of the unthinkable – is a case in point. But the vast majority of modern consultants are sorcerers. Their reputation depends on the learning acquired by study, rather than on any mystical endowment. It is the medicine that has the supernatural force, not the practitioner. In earlier business history this may well not have been true. It seems likely that the great founding fathers of consultancy like Taylor were viewed as benevolent – or malevolent (the trade unions' view of Taylor) – geniuses who had been granted flashes of supernatural insight. But the myth, as always, is difficult to disentangle from the reality; and while the Taylor of legend is, at least for his followers, a magically endowed hero-figure, this is more likely to represent latter-day accretions than the contemporary view.

As far as a typology of management sorcerers is concerned there are consultants who work as individuals, and those who are members of an institution. Both types abound in our culture, whereas in the most primitive communities the individualist dominates. But this is a function of the complexity of society rather than a reflection of a major difference in approach. At the level of complexity reached by the Ganda of

East Africa, institutionalization of sorcery had already occurred. The Ganda recognized a number of divinities, each of
which has one or more temples in different parts of the kingdom and its own set of priests. Thus they resemble the ancient
Mediterranean cultures, and it might seem to be more proper
to talk of religion rather than sorcery. But the distinction between a group of sorcerers owing allegiance to a common doctrine and the priests of an organized religion is hard to draw.

Similarly it might be better to treat, say, the practitioners of
work study consultancy as priests of a new religion rather than
as sorcerers. I am reluctant to do so because they still subscribe
rigorously to the common doctrines of the established religion
I described earlier. Even the behavioural scientists, who at one
time seemed ready to attack the orthodoxy, have in the end
failed to do so, at least in public.

The only sect that seems to have made a serious attempt to
found a new religion are the cyberneticists whose teachings
have been most completely summarized in the published work
of Stafford Beer. For them profit is stripped of its central religious significance; what counts is the survival of the organization. The organization itself – the company – is elevated to
a position of dominant mystic importance. It is no longer an
organization of individuals, but an organism in its own right,
invisible yet immanent, intangible yet real.

As I have mentioned before, this is a magical belief. As it
derives from the analogy with biological organisms it has its
roots in sympathetic magic and has matured with the philosophy of Plato and Hegel. Its links with the State religions of
both ancient and modern societies are obvious. Indeed its
major strength may lie in those very links. For if Business
Man is looking for something fresh to worship, to dedicate
himself to, then the company is as good an object as any, and
the cybernetic doctrine is convincing. As yet there is no serious
evidence of its instrumental validity, but if it manages to provide an effective and satisfactory method of achieving emotional release and identification, then its challenge to accepted
orthodoxy may well be successful.

For a while I seriously debated including the corporate planners as a possible source of a new religion. Corporate planning

as usually practised is of course simply one of the rites performed in furtherance of orthodox religion. But a handful of the more eminent consultant and academic planners – notably Erich Jantsch and Hermann Kahn – have made serious efforts to call into question the most basic of orthodox tenets – the place of profit and the existence of the company, at least in its present form.

Unfortunately they have suggested nothing to put in their place. Nothing they offer gives substantial scope for religious expression in the way that the cybernetic doctrines do. (Some of them are cyberneticists themselves, but for the moment I am concerned mostly with the ones that aren't.) Instead they appear to provide one of the few sources of agnosticism in management. Agnosticism however can hardly be classified as a religion. It has moreover throughout human history had a notable lack of human appeal. It is unlikely to achieve any greater success in management.

On the first two bases of categorization therefore consultants are sorcerers, not witches. They operate either as individuals or in groups and schools. For either case there are parallels in other cultures.

The third basis of categorization is by function – the jobs they are called upon to do. For the all-purpose consultant is a rarity in business. Most specialize in one particular role. Equally, the all-purpose sorcerer is relatively rare in other cultures. It is inherent in the nature of knowledge gained by study and experience that it should be specialist. Universal power is more likely to be the result of supernatural endowment.

The traditional role of the *witch-doctor* is exorcism. He identifies and drives away witches and other evil influences within the tribe. Belief in witches and malignant forces is necessary in any culture that insists on determinate causes and does not recognize that success or failure may simply be matters of chance. Undeserved misfortune can in such a case only be accounted for as the result of a deliberate act by a person or spirit. The witch-doctor's role is to discover and eliminate the cause.

It is a common role in management consultancy. Sometimes, as in primitive society, it is a rational and objective one.

The primitive is no fool. If his arrows do not fly straight he is first of all likely to take technical advice from a fletcher. Only if there is nothing technically wrong with the arrows will he seek magical help. Similarly much trouble-shooting consultancy in management is technical and objective. But frequently problems arise for which there is no apparent technical cause. The manager, a member of a culture that does not recognize random events, needs to find a cause. He needs a witch-doctor – an organization consultant or efficiency expert. The names change. The role remains the same.

In most cultures it is common practice to elevate principles to the status of spirits or gods. It is most familiar to us in the Graeco-Roman pantheon, where for instance love is personified as Aphrodite. Not all cultures however go as far as the Greeks and Romans in their personalization of their deities. Often the spirit/principle is worshipped in depersonalized form (as indeed was the case with the Logos of the latter-day Greeks). This seems to be generally the case in management. 'Management by Objectives' and 'Participation' are two examples of principles that have been transformed into beneficent (but still depersonalized) spirits. 'Bad organization' is an example of a malevolent one. It happens to be currently the one most in fashion as a scapegoat for otherwise unaccountable misfortune.

It is therefore the one that most frequently needs sniffing-out and exorcising. Here the witch-doctors are busiest. Objectively the formal organization of companies has a very low correlation with success or failure. One can be as loosely put together as Litton in its heyday or as impeccably structured as General Motors, with comparable results. The same company with the same organization can at one time be an overwhelming success and at another run into trouble. (Litton is again a case in point.) The manager cannot face such unaccountable fluctuations. He suspects 'bad organization', perhaps 'poor communications' or 'weak marketing', and summons a sorcerer with the appropriate medicines, which, whether or not there is any objective improvement, at least eases his mind.

Closely related to the witch-doctor is the placator of demons and external evil influences. Sometimes, as with the *peaiman* of Guyana, he is powerful enough to frighten them away. More often his role is simply to assuage and persuade. In the management culture he is paralleled by the public relations consultants (and possibly the industrial relations consultant).

PR of course has two major functions. One is to assist advertising campaigns, the other to take care of 'corporate image projection'. I am concerned with the latter. Image projection too has two major objects. The first, which normally is more important, is to increase the self-esteem of members of the company, especially its leaders. Their sense of community must be heightened and their feelings of importance and power strengthened. It is essentially magico-religious.

Such motives run counter to the accepted ethical preachings of the culture. They need an excuse and a rationalization. It is provided by the second and more common object of corporate image projection. For the most powerful of the incomprehensible forces believed to pervade the manager's world is 'public opinion'. It has various manifestations, any one of which may be given pride of place. For some the 'attitude of the Government' may be all-important. For others it is the 'attitude of the unions'. For many the figure most to be feared is 'the man in the street' – an example of anthropomorphic personalization which is exceptionally well-developed for this culture.

But whatever the manifestation that has most local importance, to have the force of public opinion turn against one is one of the worst supernatural threats. It therefore requires powerful medicine to placate it. Although many, perhaps most, companies have built up their own fund of occult knowledge, the usual practice is still to call in the outside specialist whose magic is necessarily more powerful than one's own.

A third role of major importance in any society is that of the *soothsayer,* the sorcerer whose special medicine allows him to see at least a little into the future. Such power is assumed to be congenital or supernaturally endowed. Even in the management culture, with its current predisposition to value sorcery more highly than witchcraft, there is a general belief that some individuals are gifted with managerial 'flair' or 'hunch' to predict the results of present action. However, it is largely a

relic of an earlier stage in the development of the present
culture. In all except the more backward tribes belief in flair is
reserved to the older age-groups, and admitted only with a
certain guilty defiance. In any case, as is usual with magical
phenomena, distance lends its own enchantment. I have
known, but prefer not to name, several prominent business
leaders whose flair was more apparent to the Press and the
public than to their own subordinates.

For its soothsaying therefore, management relies more and
more on the trained sorcerer – the economic forecasters and the
opinion pollsters. Both practices surround themselves with the
pseudo-scientific trappings of elementary mathematics. But
their activities are based on arbitrary assumptions that are almost certainly untrue. For the forecasters rely on the assumption that people will act in their own best interests, and the
pollsters assume that people know, or will admit, how they will
act in hypothetical circumstances. Both beliefs are beyond empirical testing (and therefore by definition magical). What is
known tends to invalidate them. It is hardly surprising that the
success record of economic and opinion forecasters seems ap-
proximately equal to that of the Delphic oracle.

Some of the more egregious failures of forecasting – the
Edsel, IPC's *Sun* – have passed into myth. As with the
Delphic oracle and primitive soothsaying in general, the error
is attributed to the interpreter who has to transmute the fore-
cast into action. Thus, in spite of the subsequent dismal failure
of IPC's *Sun*, Dr Abrams's study of the future newspaper reading public is still held up as a model of the correctly performed
forecasting ritual.

The manager, like the tribesman, is prepared to admit his
own limitations and those of his peers. But he recoils from the
thought that the future is random. He needs to believe that it is
predictable, and that some sorcerers somewhere can success-
fully predict it. And since he needs to believe, he believes.

It would be possible to compile an exhaustive list of the
various functions that sorcerers and witches fill in primitive
society and show their parallels in the management culture.
Rain-makers, for instance, ensuring crop fertility, are replaced
by the marketing consultants we bring in to ensure fertility of a

new product. But enough has already been said to establish the validity of the analogy.

In sum, the consultant is viewed as having acquired learning that gives him powers greater than ordinary mortals. He is summoned partly for the instrumental effect of his medicine but also for the cathartic satisfaction of emotional pressures, to reassure the manager that he is working in a proper manner. The worth of his actions is beyond empirical test. Where it isn't, failure is explained away as the responsibility of the manager charged to implement the recommendations. The thought that failure might be due to a flaw in the medicine itself is unacceptable.

Finally, the more distant the origin of the consultant, the stronger his medicine is supposed to be. Any consultant is more powerful than one's own staff. An American consultant working in Europe (or a European in America) is more powerful than his native-born rivals. An American who is specially flown in is more powerful still. As far as I know it hasn't happened yet, but the time cannot be far off when both American and European companies, driven by the search for more and more powerful medicine, will call in Japanese consultants. All magico-religious systems have the same law. Foreign magic is mysterious and therefore more powerful than the domestic variety.

SALES

5. Fertility Rites

One of the great charms about the small-circulation, specialist end of the magazine publishing industry is that returns can be high, while the actual cost of launching a new journal is minimal. In the extreme, it is even possible for the marginal cash flow never to be negative – payment is normally by subscription in advance and printers and promotional media are notoriously lax in their credit arrangements. (In such a situation standard measures of return on investment, discounted or not, go off wildly to infinity and lose any practical value. But I shall be returning to this topic later.) Even in the more normal run of things the investment is more likely to be measured in hundreds rather than thousands of pounds.

Moreover, to identify a market gap, compile potential subscription lists, collate editorial material and arrange for production and distribution is essentially routine and straightforward.

Yet a few years ago a director of a major international company in the field proudly showed me a critical path analysis of his company's procedures in launching a new journal. The document, especially prepared by an outside OR team, was neat, elegant, carefully worked out and impressive – until I noticed that 39 weeks had elapsed from the inception of the idea to first publication.

That figure is ridiculous. A friend in a smaller and more successful publishing house frothed slightly and snorted: 'Six weeks is enough time to get anything off the bloody ground.' I suspect he was exaggerating, though there are examples of journals launched in under six weeks. But I remain convinced that something like 30 of those 39 weeks were spent in unnecessary activity. And a market-research campaign is usually more expensive than to launch a journal.

The journals that were launched in 39 weeks could have

been launched in nine, and there is no reason to suspect that they would have been any more or less successful. Certainly that particular company's profit record was no better than anyone else's in the field (though it was quite good).

I rather diffidently pointed out that much of the activity was useless. The strength of the reaction demonstrated that while the activity might have little practical use, it nevertheless filled some kind of need. At the time I didn't really understand what need. Now it is obvious to me. Without the references to committees, the gathering of comments from existing journals in the same group, the carrying out of market research, the careful and lengthy selection of staff, the estimation of discounted-cash-flow returns and all the other things that padded out the 39 weeks, nobody in the company concerned would have felt easy in their minds.

These things had to be done, just as the obsessive neurotic has to count the steps he takes, or as the Dobuan islander has to plant charms to guard his yam crops against magical influences. They were simply magico-religious rites. In particular, fertility rites.

The primitive tribe is almost totally dependent on the vagaries of nature for its continued existence. Much of its routine magical practices are aimed at ensuring the fruitful continuance of the basic cycles of nature – the daily alternation of light and dark, the annual procession of the seasons – or at averting disasters like floods, tempests or drought that can destroy the fertility of the land on which the tribe and the animals it tends or hunts depend.

That the annual recurrence of the seasons and the spasmodic occurrence of storms and tempests should be the result of blind impersonal forces is inconceivable for the savage. He understands them to depend on the arbitrary will of some supernatural power. The savage must do whatever he can to influence that will in the right direction. Depending on the particular culture, he may attempt to constrain, coax, assuage, persuade or even bribe the spirits. To this end he will perform the rituals in which he has been brought up to believe – the ones that, after all, worked last year.

Our scientific understanding and our increased technological ability has obviated the need for magical practices even in the industries that are dependent on agriculture or seasonal effects. So proper fertility rites have no place in modern management. I have therefore appropriated the term to describe those rituals that have grown up around the phenomenon that for the modern manager has the same place as fertility for the savage. For his livelihood and success, for the continued existence of the community to which he belongs, the manager is more than anything else dependent on the generation of revenue and profit. It is reasonable therefore that this set of activities should be especially encrusted with ritual.

The greatest accretion of ritual is around those areas which present the greatest risk, and which are least understood. There are in fact two such areas, both of which have already been referred to in discussing consultants: the launch of new products, and the attempt to plan for the future.

I have already touched upon the subject of new launches in the opening of this chapter. That example was extreme in the sense that the lack of practical utility of most of the activities surrounding the launch was immediately obvious. Normally it is harder to disentangle the reality from the rationalization. But in other respects the example is typical.

Let us consider for a moment what happens when a new product is to be launched. In principle the process is much the same everywhere. A market opportunity is identified, or a new product is invented. The rituals begin with the presentation of the idea to management for decision. Broadly speaking, management has to make three decisions – whether to produce or not, how much to produce, and what price to sell it at.

Making the decisions depends on four questions. How much will it cost to produce? How many people will buy it? What price will they pay? And what will that represent in terms of profit?

I would myself contend that the questions are each un-answerable – if the first three are, the last must be – in any deterministic sense. Partly this may be due to the ineffective-ness of the techniques we have at our disposal, but I see no evidence to indicate that our techniques are likely to get any better in the future. Granted we now have much more complex and sophisticated techniques than our forebears. But our performance record in making money out of new products is no better. (In many cases it is much worse – compare Dupont's Corfam with Dupont's nylon.)

However, in the management culture my view is heretical. For the manager in general the questions can be answered, and must be answered, just as questions about the after-life have had to be answered by religions from time immemorial. Let us look therefore at his attempts to answer them.

How much will the new product cost? The manager faced with the decision will approach the heads of his production, engineering and personnel departments for estimates. (For the sake of ritual purity, he will be aided by the ubiquitous accountant.) They in turn will subdivide the task among their subordinates until somewhere down the line someone who is either naïve or vain, or has no one else to turn to, will make a guess. Ultimately the guesses will be added together. (The accountant will make sure the addition is correct, and that the various sums are properly charged to the appropriate cost centres). The result is presented to the decision-maker. It is impossible to accept, even before the Rolls-Royce disaster, that anyone thought that this process could ever produce an accurate answer.

But the manager believes there must be an answer. So the ritual must be religiously adhered to. An avowed guess by the decision-maker himself is not enough, even though it has as much chance of proving correct as the summation of guesses by a large number of anonymous and low-status subordinates. (There are of course some companies that do operate on the basis of accepting one man's hunches, and on the whole they are as successful as their more puritanical rivals. But they are shunned as heretics.)

My point is not that we cannot get a reasonably good idea of how much a new product will cost. Usually we can. To cost out a small circulation magazine ought to take half an hour for anyone in the business. But where a good experience-based guess of that kind is possible – in a totally new field it isn't – no amount of extra finicking is likely to increase the possibility that the estimate will prove correct. It may even worsen it.

Of course, some people are better guessers than others. They can be trained in the art, just as bridge players can be trained to assess their hands more accurately. And there are some useful ploys, like making 'at best' and 'at worst' estimates and allowing generous margins to counteract known biases towards optimism or pessimism. Beyond that the randomness of events is bound to destroy any increase of accuracy.

All that is left is luck. The only defence against luck is ritual. It is unfortunate that the business rituals for this situation are so much more time-consuming and expensive than the equally effective methods of crossing one's fingers or finding a black cat and spitting.

How much will the customer buy, and at what price? Volume and price are obviously linked, though not with the monotonic simplicity taught by economists. Sometimes a rise in price produces an increase in sales, and a cut sometimes produces a decrease. There are occasions when a change in price produces no change at all in volume. In classical terms, the elasticity of demand can be negative or zero, at least in limited ranges.

Nevertheless it remains true that demand is influenced, albeit imperfectly, by price. It follows that there must be at least one price level at which sales reach a maximum, and another level at which profit reaches a maximum. (The levels may occasionally be identical.) The art therefore is to estimate what the level of demand will be at various price levels, and then to calculate which level will produce the greatest profit.

The theory is elegant, simple and convincing. The trouble is it doesn't work. Looking back we can always say: 'We had to turn away customers, so if we'd only priced it higher we could have made more money.' Or we can say: 'We were only working at half-capacity – if we'd charged less we'd have done better.' But the theory only works in retrospect. And as it's always possible to demonstrate that a pricing decision could have been improved on, the attempt is made to apply the system in advance – just as in cost estimation the accounting principles that developed to record historical cost are used to eliminate future uncertainty.

Unfortunately however there are only two ways to estimate

what the price-demand curve is likely to be. One is to test-market – to put the product on sale in a limited area and see what happens. It has the undeniable merit of being empirical and scientific, but probably for that very reason it is frequently unacceptable. It is of course also expensive. So to ease his doubts and fears the manager is driven back on to the only other method – market research. The idea behind market research is that if you want to know how the customer is going to react, you ask him.

Again, it is simple, logical and sensible enough. Just as it was simple, logical and sensible enough to ask the war-god to indicate, via the entrails of a chicken, whether he was favourably disposed towards a particular campaign. The Roman priests were suffering from the false assumption that there was a war-god who determined the outcome of battles. The market researcher suffers from the mistaken belief that the customer can predict how he himself will behave, or that he will tell the truth. In fact, most people understand their own motivations so badly that they are incapable of predicting their behaviour. In any case the producer-customer relationship is such that all the pressures on the customer are to lie, especially on the price question.

In defence against this criticism, it is usually claimed that the researcher questions hundreds, perhaps thousands, of customers. The errors will therefore 'cancel out'. It sounds good. It does a great deal to bolster the confidence of the manager that in commissioning market research he is doing the right thing. As an argument it is invalid on two counts.

In the first place, it entails the assumption that there is an average response around which the actual responses will be randomly distributed. There is a parallel. In assessing the average height of a population one assumes that any given individual is as likely to be above average height as below. Here errors do cancel out, and the bigger the sample the more accurate the estimate of the average. Unfortunately the responses to market researchers appear to be uniformly biased, not randomly. In such a situation enlarging the sample is no help.

Even if the falsehoods were randomly distributed, the best one could hope for would be an accurate estimate of the average honest response. And as that is more than likely to be based on misunderstanding, increasing the sample size can only focus more sharply on a wrong answer.

The idea of increasing the sample size is not new. The more important the decision facing a Roman, the more chickens he consulted.

Everything I have said about the use of market research in a pricing decision is equally true in any other situation where the work is extended to cover anything but the recording of objectively measurable factors. The number of two-car families in a neighbourhood, the types of paperback bought by railway or air passengers, the statistical distribution of shoe-size among adult males in the U K, the number and location of housewives with automatic washing machines – such matters are reasonably reliable. Preference for safety or speed in cars, intention to buy mini-, midi- or maxi-skirts, or any expression of future attitude particularly where socially approved norms are involved, are statistics with no solid ground beneath them at all.

That market research can be totally misleading is a fact of life that even the management culture cannot ignore any more than the primitive can ignore the fact that the most careful performance of fertility rites frequently results in a poor crop. But they can of course explain it away.

Rationalizations of this kind often find expression in myth, legendary tales with or without any historical foundation. They provide the rationale on which a particular ritual is based and justify occasional failures. In the management culture, and in the particular context of market research, perhaps the most widespread myth is that of the Ford Edsel.

According to the tale as it is told at seminars and conferences, after the Second World War Ford were determined to re-establish the market position which the Model T had given them a generation before. They strove to ensure that no part of all the necessary rituals would be overlooked. In particular they mounted a massive market-research campaign designed to discover what Americans would be looking for in a car they would buy by the million.

Hundreds – the number rather depends on the storyteller –

of emissaries went around the country asking citizens what would be the chief characteristics of their ideal car. They were told it would be powerful – but so as to ensure safety, not speed. It would be modest and practical, not ostentatious. It would have plenty of room for the family and for luggage. It would be easy to drive and easy to park.

So the Ford emissaries went away and told their designers what they had learned. The designers went away and came up with a car that had all the right qualities. And the Ford management slept easily, secure in the belief that they were 'market-oriented' and therefore secure from harm.

But meanwhile the minions of General Motors had also been scouring the country and seeking out the thoughts of the people. They did not ask 'What would you like to see in your ideal car?' Instead they asked 'What would your neighbour like to see?' And wherever they went they were told: 'Oh, he would like a car that looks even faster than it is, decorated with shining chromium and so eye-catching that you turn your head as it passes you on the road. He doesn't care whether it's safe, or comfortable, or whether he can cram his wife and children into it: just so long as it's impressive.'

So General Motors came up with a very different car and Ford lost several hundred million dollars.

I make no claims for the historical accuracy of the story. I have told it as I have heard it many times. The function of myth is not to record but to teach and explain. The Edsel myth teaches that Ford performed the rituals and still failed. The flaw was not in the ritual, but in the interpretation. So too the ancient Greeks told of Croesus consulting the oracle at Delphi. He was assured that if he attacked the Persians he would destroy an empire. He attacked and destroyed his own empire. The fault was not in the oracle but in him. He misinterpreted.

Over the last generation belief in the principle of 'market-orientation' has become a major dogma of the orthodox management culture. The logic, again, is simple. It is better to produce what the market wants than to insist on selling what one likes to produce. Therefore one should find out what the market wants, rather than work out new ways of selling what one has got. The first attitude is 'market-oriented' and ensures success. The second approach is 'product-oriented' and inevitably leads to failure.

That is what the creed preaches. Unfortunately the world has as many successful product-oriented companies and failed market-oriented companies as it has examples of the opposite. The correlation between market-orientation and success appears to be insignificant. (Nothing as crassly empirical as controlled testing has been allowed to mar the logical impeccability of the theory.)

Again, this is a situation that has to be explained away. But the myth I am now going to quote is subtler than those of the Edsel or of Croesus. I first heard this tale from a director of the Beecham Group, the company concerned, so it may have more historical standing than the Ford story. The important thing is that the tale is told as an example of how an impressive success has been due to market orientation.

The tale starts with the intention of the Beecham Group to launch its MacLeans toothpaste, an established success in Britain, on the American market. The necessary rituals were observed. A large sample of potential customers were invited to make a blindfold taste test of MacLeans and another unnamed American toothpaste. The overwhelming majority of the testers preferred the American toothpaste (no matter which particular brand was used).

Beecham's reaction was inspired. American toothpaste advertising at the time was centred around taste-appeal. In that contest MacLeans was obviously not going to get anywhere. But no American toothpaste was seriously advertising what presumably should be its major purpose – cleaning teeth. So Beecham's did nothing to alter the flavour of their product, but started an advertising campaign based solely around the superior power of MacLeans as a cleaner of teeth. And while it didn't exactly run away with the market, it did carve itself out a useful and profitable 15–20 per cent.

Thus the superiority of market-orientation is demonstrated.

Of course it isn't. But the day I first heard that story, told in the heady atmosphere of a warmed-up management prayer-meeting, virtually everyone present was convinced. Later that night I was up until the early hours arguing with two notable academics. I tried to point out to them that the story, if anything, shows how a good sales team can make a product-oriented company successful. In insisting on selling the product they had, rather than altering it to suit the new customers, Beecham's were by definition acting in a product-oriented way.

But I failed to win my argument, confounded by the logic that says: 'To be successful, one has to be market-oriented. Beecham's were successful, therefore what they did must have been market-oriented. Therefore what on earth are you carrying on about?'

Eventually I shut up. I wanted to point out that this line of thought does no more than define 'market-oriented' as 'associated with success', and that to be of any use at all the 'market-oriented' attitude must be identifiable *a priori*, and not simply diagnosed *ex post facto*. I gave up because I was beginning to recognize that this was a religious argument, not an empirical one.

The fourth question to be asked in launching a new product is 'How much profit will it make?' Obviously this question can be answered satisfactorily only if the first three are settled accurately. Yet even people who are sceptical of the rituals by which answers to the first three are obtained will still expend time and energy in the meticulous determination of profit projections. The literature of investment analysis is vast. It is frequently intelligent and acute, just as the scholastic philosophizing of the twelfth and thirteenth centuries is intelligent and acute. The search for greater and greater precision in making investment decisions has even led the accountancy profession into relatively high-level mathematics. The theory of discounted-cash-flow calculations involves the solution of high-degree polynomial equations, and therefore a branch of mathematics that was first fully explored less than 200 years ago.

But where the very existence of angels is in doubt, debating how many of them can dance on a pin seems a sterile exercise. Where the validity of one's original information is suspect, performing ever more sophisticated calculations seems pointless. Nonetheless, there can hardly be a company in which new projects are not required to be subjected to a ritual calculation of the 'internal rate of return', 'net present value', 'payback period' or some other criterion of profitability. And yet most of the time the performers themselves are not convinced of the validity of the material information they are manipulating. The fallibility of cost and revenue projection is widely recognized. Moreover, it is an unavoidable though unpleasant truth that where a company lays down profitability criteria for new investment, projects are always made to conform to those criteria.

If a company decides it will only go ahead with projects that show a discounted return on investment of better than 15 per cent, anyone putting forward a project will ensure that the accompanying figures indicate a better than 15 per cent return. If the criterion is raised to 20 per cent, the figures will be improved accordingly. And there is no way in which the person analysing the project can contest those figures – unless he can find a flaw in the performance of the projection rituals.

The analyses are performed even when the performers themselves will admit that they have no empirical validity. Their major function is therefore evident. They form an expressive, emotionally satisfying pattern of rituals.

Summarizing what I have said about the launch of new products, the position is clear. Faced with the necessity of answering questions that are essentially unanswerable, the manager develops a set of behaviour patterns that serve to ease his fears and his conscience. He also develops a rationale, sometimes expressed in myth, that explains his behaviour and justifies failures. It is the way mankind has always behaved in similar circumstances.

As I pointed out earlier in the chapter, the second major area in which this type of behaviour manifests itself is in the related field of planning. Again, mankind has always planned and needed to plan. In spite of the New Testament injunction very few have been willing to imitate the lilies of the field in their unconcern for the future. Those content to live only for the satisfaction of present desires have been classified as insane, immoral or retarded. In current terminology, such a response to life is psychopathic. Equally 'abnormal' is the person who, although he admits concern about the future, is pessimistic or discouraged enough to do nothing about it. To be concerned about the future necessitates trying to do something about it. It requires planning. For any kind of rational activity to take place, one must know what one is trying to achieve and how one intends to achieve it.

The concept applies as much to the management of businesses as to any other activity. All businesses indeed do plan. The differences between them are only matters of extent, degree, style and length of time they are prepared to look ahead.

Unfortunately no one has been prepared to leave it at that simple a level. In the ceaseless search for guarantees of success the word 'planning' has been transformed from a noun identifying a rational activity into an incantation. So have derivative phrases like 'corporate planning', 'business planning', 'long-range planning,' 'strategic planning', 'entrepreneurial planning' etc.

The activity itself has been transformed from a rational matter of sensibly deciding what to do into a complex pattern of behaviour, the pragmatic value of which is minimal. The pattern varies in detail from company to company, partly because of local circumstance, partly dependent on the school of thought the company adheres to. For as a part of the managerial structure of beliefs planning has been long enough entrenched for rival sects to have emerged. Each is prepared to defend fiercely its particular version of the proper way to behave. They are agreed only in the belief that a company that does not consciously and overtly plan has no future worth speaking of.

This makes it difficult to offer a description of what happens in a 'typical' company. The best I can do is present a composite picture drawn from what happens in several companies I happen to know, and note some of the points where rival sects would recommend different action.

The fictitious company has several different products and is organized into divisions, each of which has profit responsibility. Its planning 'cycle' is annual – a virtually universal characteristic. It has no long range plans. (In many schools of thought plans must be made further ahead than this. In the

vast majority of cases the period prescribed is five years – for
no better reason than that, in the decimal system, five and ten
have replaced three and seven as the most common mystic
numbers.)

Each year, therefore, the board of directors meets and ap-
proves target profit figures for the entire company. They are
prepared and submitted by the managing director. Each year
these figures are prepared on a different basis – by considering
what would look good in the annual report, for instance, or
what competitors are doing, or what would rescue the company from the danger of take-over. (Almost any sect of planners would be horrified by this situation: they all have their
own formulae for determining initial targets. What has been
happening in this company is that it has been rapidly passing
through one school of thought after another.)

After approval the managing director breaks the figures into
profit targets for each division. They are then passed on to the
division heads, with a request for the submission of a plan to
achieve them. (A diametrically opposed school of thought favours initial submission of targets *by* each division; and there
are other variants.) The division heads consult their own staffs
and submit plans which, typically, amount to about 20 per cent
less than they have been asked for. Each division head, who is
of course a member of the board that approved the original
targets, has his own method of preparing the divisional plan.
The methods range from guessing to sophisticated analysis of
what is happening in the markets he serves, what plans he has
for diversification or expansion, what trade union action there
is likely to be, and so on. It makes little difference to the
general rule of a 20 per cent discount, except for the fact that
one division regularly returns a plan for exactly meeting the
suggested target, as long as it is allowed to do several things
it has already been forbidden to do. Most of them require
large amounts of capital investment.

There ensue several weeks of debate, discussion, confrontation, recrimination and sometimes abuse. At the end the divisional plans are accepted, and the original overall targets are
scaled down by 20 per cent. A total 'corporate plan' is assem-
bled and approved by the board of directors.

By this time the planned year has already started. By the time four or five months have gone by it is obvious that the plan will not be achieved. It is scrapped. The managing director's staff is instructed to start preparing a plan for the following year.

In some companies targets are met or even exceeded. In others they are missed. There is, unfortunately, no apparent distinction in planning method or degree of sophistication between the successful companies and the failures.

But the theory is excellent. The company determines the objectives that should be achieved during the next planning period, these are broken down into separate objectives for each part of the organization, different individuals are given the responsibility for achieving those objectives, and the authority and power to do so. It ought to work. It is so convincing that the creed of 'management by objectives' is almost as widely held as the dogma that the purpose of business is to make a profit. So why does it fail?

Partly because of the difficulties in forecasting that I have already mentioned, but this effect is small since it only applies to new ventures. Forecasting is relatively easy in the case of an ongoing product. Much more importantly the theory is doomed to failure from the very beginning because of a basic fallacy that strikes at the very heart of the management religion. The creed says that the purpose of a company is to maximize profit. Therefore corporate plans are invariably cast in terms of profit or some equivalent – after-tax earnings, dividend-plus-retained-earnings, return on capital employed are obvious examples. If at all, this assumption is true only for owner-managed businesses. The true motives of the directors of any other kind of business only include the maximization of profit as a secondary item – at best.

Such objectives as are committed to paper are masks for the true, if not always consciously admitted, objectives of the participants. They are ritualistic expressions of good intent, made because society demands them rather than because of any genuine desire to achieve them. They are held to only in so far as they do not clash with any of the true objectives of the people concerned.

No other interpretation is consistent with the fact that failure to achieve the planned target is very, very rarely punished. Making an egregious loss may be punished. Activity that brings the company into disrepute may be punished. Actions that offend the senior directorate will certainly be. Refusal to take part in the formalities of the planning procedure will be. But failure to meet any particular target will as often as not go unnoticed, except perhaps by the bureaucracy that develops to administer the plan.

In the meantime most people's planning effort will go into working out how they can achieve their own personal aims. The contribution they make, or promise to make, to the corporate plan will depend entirely on how it fits into their own personal strategy.

It may be difficult to see why corporate planning has become so widespread, and why the particular groups of sorcerers who devote themselves to the practice have become so universally popular. But the difficulty vanishes as soon as the activity is viewed in its proper light, not as an act expected to have pragmatic validity, but as an expressive and placatory ritual.

Some managers take part in corporate planning purely cynically, as a sixteenth-century agnostic might go to church. It is the expected thing to do, and one can expect social ostracism for not conforming to the dogma. Others take part because they are convinced by the arguments and because they have faith in the superior powers of the people who advocate it. For them it is a ritual that expresses their faith. It cements their membership in the modern management community.

Both groups would abandon the system were a more emotionally satisfying one to present itself and become generally adopted. But there is a small though fervent group of people who do believe that the setting of corporate objectives in the ritually approved manner does somehow help to ensure their achievement. Their fallacy is perhaps the oldest of all. It relates closely to sympathetic magic, in which the performance of one action ensures the occurrence of a similar one. It finds its earliest expression among the Stone Age artists who painted on the walls of their caves pictures of the animals they intended to kill, and the way in which they planned to hunt them.

It is an interesting sidelight on the universality of human behaviour patterns that the earliest written records we have should be those of a corporate plan.

6. Controlling the Elements

The same general patterns of behaviour can be identified through the whole range of human societies, but any culture taken on its own can be expected to provide certain unique aspects. Thus the massive human sacrifices that typify some pre-Columbian American societies have only occasional echoes elsewhere. Few if any other cultures are as placidly unemotional as the Pueblo Indians. Nowhere except in the Judaeo-Christian tradition is there such a sense of the sinfulness of sexual relations.

As with the three cases quoted, it is not always easy to see why the unique aspects should have developed. Often however special circumstances in the environment provide a reasonably simple explanation. This is true of the set of management rituals I want to discuss in this chapter.

Tribes will develop a complex set of rituals to control the particular elemental forces on which they depend. So does the management culture. For the manager by definition is dependent on his ability to get other people to work for him. He depends on their labour in much the same way as the fisherman depends on the sea, or the ancient Egyptians depended on the Nile. And in the entire environment that surrounds the manager, the most unpredictable, least understood and least controllable factor is the behaviour of the people he manages. Not surprisingly, therefore, the subject is shrouded with mystique.

It is also an area in which a major convulsion has taken place during the last decade or so. At times it has almost reached the dimensions of the bitter disputation following the clash between Darwin's evolutionary theory and the doctrines of Christian Fundamentalism. It too arose from the scientific pursuit of a line of inquiry that threatened some of the basic axioms of the accepted structure of social beliefs, – in this case particularly the belief that the motivation of man at work is purely economic. Is monetary reward the only satisfaction that man seeks from his job, and does it offer sufficient inducement to make him perform his tasks well?

It was denied in the writings of psychologists and sociologists, mainly American, who in the post-war period laid the foundations of what was to be called 'Behavioural Science'. As the quotation marks and capital letters indicate, to me this is a perversion of the words. Just as Evolution with a capital E has come to mean the Darwinian theory, so Behavioural Science has in popular usage come to denote the theory of these writers.

Their thesis is hard to dispute. A few minutes' honest introspection would lead anyone to agree that the effort he puts into his work is only minimally related to the monetary reward involved. It isn't immediately understandable, therefore, why the teachings of the Behavioural Scientists were not quickly accepted – let alone why they generated such passionate argument and even persecution. There exist companies in which the taint of belief in Behavioural Science is enough to debar a manager from further promotion and to make him more liable to redundancy than his orthodox colleagues. In other companies to profess belief in the new teaching is a *sine qua non* of keeping one's job, let alone gaining advancement.

The unreasonable violence of the reaction, in relation to the relative modesty of the original observation, demands explanation. It can only come from an examination of the essential managerial beliefs.

Traditionally the world of the manager was well-structured. People's roles and their relationships to one another were well-defined, and their motives straightforward. There was a clear hierarchy. The manager knew his place, knew the way in which he was expected to behave and what to expect of his superiors and his subordinates. In return for 'a fair day's pay' one gave 'a fair day's work'. The same principle applied whether one was paid literally on a daily basis, or for some longer term. The concept of 'a fair day's work' included loyalty, dedication and effort, as well as the meticulous performance of allotted tasks.

There was a typical confusion of fact and belief. The concept was not only held to describe how things were, but more importantly, how they ought to be. Managers, no matter how traditional their beliefs, would admit that some individuals did not give 'a fair day's work' for their 'fair day's pay'. But they would view them as violators of the proper code, sinners, and as such deserving only of punishment.

Against that background it is easier to understand why a lot of managers reacted violently against Behavioural Science teaching. It suggested that a majority of people found the traditional economic bargain insufficient, and instead of being punished they should be rewarded in new and different ways. It was like suggesting that sexual profligacy or drug addiction should not only be forgiven but encouraged.

Workers and their trade union representatives were equally incensed. I once read a letter from a middle-aged shop steward to his managing director who had been attempting to introduce more enlightened practices of consultation and participation into his company. Unfortunately I cannot quote it verbatim, but it was an eloquent protest against the very idea that the company should be concerned with the individual's need or desire for companionship, for esteem, for self-realization, or any other of the motivating forces that, according to the Behavioural Scientists, are more important than money. In his view such things were the proper preserve of the individual himself. For the company to take them into account was, quite simply, morally wrong. It had, in his own phrase, no 'right' to do so.

It is unlikely that many managers would have analysed their violent reaction against the new heresy in this way. Confronted with an ill-defined feeling that it was somehow 'wrong', they were more likely to challenge its validity, to dismiss it as 'poppycock', 'idealist', or 'unworkable'. And with that bland disregard for objectivity possible only to the religious believer, any evidence to the contrary would be ignored. In some cases the implementation of Behavioural Science teaching in a company had actually improved the company's profit record. But such news tended to be received with scepticism and explained away as the result of some local abnormality in the particular company's environment.

The converts who rushed to the Behavioural Science banner, however, transformed what had originally been a set of reasonably empirical findings into something more akin to a religious creed. But before looking at them in detail it is worthwhile describing rather more fully the beliefs they subscribed to.

Not surprisingly, the origin of the Behavioural Science movement is now enshrined in myth, in particular the great myth of the Hawthorne Experiment. (Whether this event, which actually took place, should really be called an experiment, or whether any other trimmings to the story are factually accurate or not, is immaterial.) In its essentials the tale is a short one. Once upon a time, in the late twenties, a company called Western Electric commissioned consultants to carry out studies in its Hawthorne plant in Chicago in an attempt to increase productivity. The investigators chose a part of the plant called the Bank Wiring Room, and as a first step they increased its illumination. Output went up. In order to quantify the effect, they then reduced the lighting. Output went up again. What had happened, according to the legend, was that the workers in the room were working harder because for once someone was taking an interest in them. They felt more important. As a result they were more 'motivated'.

It may seem improbable that a revolution in managerial thinking should spread from such a little incident. But just as minor were the mythical encounters of St Francis and Gautama Buddha. And the relatively simple experiments conducted by Michelson and Morley swept away the apparently eternal truths of Newtonian physics.

Whatever the truth of the Hawthorne myth, in the forties and fifties a series of scientists attempted to analyse and describe the various factors that lead people to work productively. Among the earliest was Abraham Maslow. His major contribution was the postulate that each individual has a hierarchy of needs which he attempts to satisfy. They range from the basic physiological needs for food and drink through the need for shelter, companionship, esteem, up to the highest, the need for 'self-actualization'. Only as each level of need is satisfied

does the next higher come into play. Once a need is satisfied it
no longer acts to motivate the individual concerned. Mid-twen-
tieth century man, Maslow said, has been effectively cushioned
by society. Unlike his ancestors, he is no longer primarily
driven by his lower-level needs. To induce him to work harder
managers must therefore help him fulfil his higher-level needs.

Variations on that (over-simplified) message were produced
by others, notably Likert, McClelland, McGregor (whom I
have already mentioned in the Introduction), Argyris, and
Herzberg. The most successful in Britain has undoubtedly been
Frederick Herzberg, the inventor of 'job enrichment'. Herzberg's creed is relatively simple. He divides the various factors
that lead people to work into two kinds. The first, which he
calls 'hygiene' factors, include pay and comfort. If absent, they
cause trouble, but as long as they are adequate they go unnoticed. The manager must make sure that these factors are
satisfactorily provided for. But at best they produce an attitude
of neutrality in the worker. For inducing positive effort, the
manager has to turn to the second category, which Herzberg
calls 'motivating' factors. They include responsibility, interest,
and job-satisfaction.

The hygiene factors are concerned with the environment of
the job, whereas the motivating factors are elements of the job
itself. To improve his workers' attitudes the manager must
alter the job itself. He must enrich it.

During this period a great deal of valuable scientific work
was done in America and elsewhere to establish empirically
what does account for the fact that different people work with
varying degrees of effort and dedication, and that the same
people work harder in some situations than in others. However, most of the research was successful only in that it de-
molished cherished preconceptions. Investigating a group of
East Anglian factories Joan Woodward, for instance, established that there is no apparent correlation between success
and conformity to the strict classical rules of organization. But
while a number of people, including those named, have come
up with theories that explain the results of their own experiments, no one has yet produced a theory that has any tested
predictive value. As yet we have no evidence that the

introduction of what are called 'Behavioural Science principles' is necessarily either good or bad for a company in terms of economic success.

Of course there are examples of companies that have changed their management styles and been successful, but no more than counter-instances of companies that have changed and failed, or stayed traditional and succeeded. Failures can be, and are, explained away on the basis that the managements concerned 'weren't really' practising what they preached. This kind of *ex post facto* rationalization indicates strongly that the 'Behavioural Science' movement has lost its original empiricism.

There is no incontestable way of demonstrating that any particular method of managing a company is superior in producing efficiency. Therefore changing belief must be viewed as a religious phenomenon.

Comparisons with other cultures are informative. One valuable study has been carried out by Raymond Firth on the Polynesian island of Tikopia. Over the period of a generation or more he was able to analyse the conversion of the Tikopians from a mostly pagan society to an almost completely Christian one. From discussing with converts their reasons for changing beliefs he identified ten equally important factors. (Only one of them is irrelevant to the process of changing managerial style. At least as far as I am aware, dreams, which were frequently given by the Tikopians as a reason for conversion, have not played a significant part among managers.)

The first of the reasons for change is economic benefit. Some Tikopians felt that by becoming Christian they would share in the prosperity of the Europeans. Similarly many managers adopted Behavioural Science beliefs because, as known experts in a new field, they hoped to increase their prospects for advancement, and consequently their prosperity. Note one point. This is not an expression of belief in the superiority of either Christianity or Behavioural Science, but a conviction that professed Christians on the one hand, and professed Behavioural Scientists on the other, would be treated better by those in authority.

Conviction of the truth of Christian theology and morality

was another factor. Professor Firth considered that though 'this rarely if ever operated alone to secure conversion, nevertheless its importance should not be underestimated'. As far as Behavioural Science is concerned, many managers were intellectually persuaded by the logic of the various sects, plus the apparently empirical basis of their teaching. But intellectual persuasion on its own rarely produces any change in behaviour.

Conviction is different from 'yielding to dogmatic argument'. The Tikopians were affected by the Christian promise of a life hereafter. Behavioural Scientists often presented life in a traditional company as a minor hell in comparison with the delights of life in a company that is 'participation-oriented'. And many managers adopted the Behavioural Science viewpoint, not because they thought it correct, but because it seemed to offer a more pleasant life.

Then there is another factor, conformity to external authority. As Professor Firth says,

Until recent years the Tikopians were so conscious of their technological inferiority that they were prepared to be impressed by any outsider who claimed to know the true way of doing things. Consequently, the claim that Christianity was the right form of religious belief and practice in the modern world was one that many Tikopians found it hard to resist.

To anyone involved with British industry over the last decade that statement must have an obvious analogy. Behavioural Science as a creed was essentially American, and therefore had all the external authority that things American gain from the obvious superiority of American business. But even in the US itself Behavioural Science was from the outset associated with the more glamorous industries (computers, software, microminiaturization) and gained authority from that connection.

Obedience to internal authority plays an equally important role. As one Tikopian explained, 'When our father became a Christian, we all followed suit: not a person could abstain.' The Tikopian referred to his chief, not his literal father. Many managers adopted Behavioural Science simply because their bosses had. The principle of *cujus regio, ejus religio* which settled the religious wars of the Reformation is still valid in modern business.

The hope of attaining increased status through conversion is said to have been relatively unimportant among the Tikopians. But it is important to a great many managers, especially senior managers and directors, for whom the thought of being in the forefront of managerial progress, and being known to be so, was irresistible.

The Tikopians were also attracted by the corporate life of the Church community. 'Membership offered daily assembly and singing, full participation in Saints' Day celebrations, dances, initiation, rites of baptism, marriage rites and a general sense of "belonging" to a wide organization reaching out beyond Tikopia and the Solomons to the lands of the Europeans.' In immediate social activity, that of course goes far beyond anything Behavioural Science had to offer. But it would be a mistake to underestimate the feeling of fellowship created by attending seminars and conferences, by sharing an esoteric jargon and being part of a group working towards common ends.

A related reason for conversion distinguished by Professor Firth is the magnetism of a mass movement. By the later sixties this was beginning to be a factor in managers' conversion to Behavioural Science, especially among the young. But since Behavioural Science still has not managed to achieve the allegiance, even outwardly, of a majority of the society, the importance of this factor is not yet as great as it may become.

Much the same is true of the final factor – unease at the religious division of the community. Nevertheless some managers have adopted the principles of Behavioural Science because they felt, if finding themselves in an orthodox minority, that unanimity of belief is essential to a company's well-being. 'Rocking the boat' goes so deeply against most managers' codes of behaviour, that outward conformity to a set of beliefs not genuinely held is preferable to appearing to be a dissenter.

Thus we find a close analogy between the process of accepting the principles of Behavioural Science and the process of religious conversion. As always, we will find among the converts a large number of individuals whose adherence to the new beliefs is merely verbal. They may ritually mouth the prescribed forms of support for such concepts as trusting subordinates, encouraging independence and widening responsibilities, but still behave in exactly the way they did before conversion.

I once ran a series of courses for senior managers on the principles of Behavioural Science. After a year or so I closed it down, as it gradually became clear that all we had succeeded in doing was educating people to make more and more sophisticated excuses for behaving in the same way they had always done.

Typical of the products of these courses – and most other educational programmes in Behavioural Science that have been carried out in industry in the last few years – was a personnel director who claimed to be a confirmed believer in McGregor's Theory Y. 'But,' he always added, 'to make Theory Y work you have to use Theory X.' The blatant paradox inherent in such a remark, and the logical impossibility of his position, was beyond him. Yet he was rarely contradicted, mainly because his superiors and colleagues were reassured that he was unlikely actually to do anything revolutionary, and his subordinates were too subdued by his extrovert temper to dare gainsay him.

He was in precisely the same position as the Crusader attempting to spread the doctrines of pacifism by the use of the sword. Whatever his motives for expressing belief in the new faith, they cannot have been a sincere adoption of its teachings.

Such people however expect to derive benefit from their 'conversion'. In return for repeating the formulae of the new ritual, they expect the promised rewards to flow in their direction. Attribution of power to incantations and spells alone is one of the major characteristics of a magico-religious cult. It is one of the most convincing demontrations that, whatever its origins, 'Behavioural Science' as it developed in industry in the sixties was a magico-religious, not a scientific, movement.

7. Rites of Passage

'In some tribes the novice is considered dead, and he remains dead for the duration of his novitiate. It lasts for a fairly long time and consists of a physical and mental weakening which is undoubtedly intended to make him lose all recollection of his childhood existence. Then follows the positive part: instruction in tribal law and a gradual education as the novice witnesses totem ceremonies, recitations of myths, etc. The final act is a religious ceremony ... and, above all, a special mutilation which varies with the tribe ... and which makes the novice forever identical with the adult members.'

This quotation from the distinguished French anthropologist Arnold van Gennep describes the initiation of an Australian aborigine into his totem group. It is simply an example of the most widespread of all types of ritual. Van Gennep christened such rituals *rites de passage*, and the literal English translation has become the standard term.

In all societies, from the simplest to the most complex, the individuals change status and role as they progress through life. At its most basic level, the child becomes a man, the man grows old and dies. And at each transitional point ceremonial acts are required, not merely to record but also to justify and institutionalize the change. Perhaps the most familiar of such rites are the Christian sacraments of baptism, confirmation and extreme unction.

As society grows more complex, the roles of its members become more sharply differentiated, and the categories into which they are grouped become more numerous. As a result, the transitions of the individual from one category to another multiply, necessitating an increase in the number and variety of rites of passage. The institutions of marriage and priesthood add two sacraments. The existence of secret societies in West Africa requires the development of rituals to mark membership.

While rites of passage are celebrated everywhere, the forms vary. So do their overt purposes and their interpretations. Sometimes they are seen as ways of eliminating evil, of purifying the new members. Sometimes they are methods of testing the fitness or acceptability of the candidate. Sometimes they are incantations designed to avert ill luck. There are even rational, instrumental interpretations, as when the ceremonies include a period of training in the skills considered necessary to success in the society. (Whether the skills are objectively necessary is not particularly relevant. The training period may well include instruction in building a canoe and in casting spells to make it go faster – to the primitive the two things are of the same kind.)

Van Gennep collected examples of the rites of passage. He also established that all such rites contain three elements, normally consecutive. Rites of separation are followed by rites of transition, and then by rites of incorporation. The individual must first be separated from his previous environment, then spend some time in a transitional, neutral state, and finally be incorporated into his new environment. Frequently, as in the mysteries of classical Greece and Rome, the first and last of these three stages are symbolized as death and rebirth, with the transitional stage equivalent to existence in Limbo.

Since rites of passage exist in all societies, it would be surprising not to find them in management. True, management, mysteries of classical Greece and Rome, the first and last of his maturity only. Nonetheless it is a hierarchical structure, and moving from one category to another in the hierarchy is so important that it cannot pass without ceremony. Apart from the hierarchical categories, management is sub-divided occupationally, and the establishment of an individual as a member of a particular occupational group is also an occasion for ritual – thus becoming an accountant involves rites of passage, as we have seen in a previous chapter. Rites of transition from one occupation to another, however, have not become commonly established. The event is too rare. It is very difficult for a manager to transfer from one occupational caste (say marketing) to another (say purchasing). The way in which job advertisements religiously insist on previous experience is evidence enough. Undoubtedly this is due as much to a feeling of the sanctity of caste barriers as to practical considerations.

Before looking at the rites of passage up the managerial hierarchy, it is probably worth considering the categories (or 'ranks') separate enough for the passage from one to another to demand ceremonial recognition.

Leaving aside the office of Chief Executive (chairman, president, managing director) itself, the highest category is the directorate. In Britain this is normally equivalent to the Board of Directors of a company. In the U S, where large boards with a majority of 'outside' members are more common, the parallel is less exact. However, I will use the term 'directorate' to refer to the group of senior executives who report directly to the chief executive. In the U S they will probably be called Vice-Presidents.

The next group I should like to call 'general management'. In some companies this group may be equivalent to the directorate, in others the two overlap. In other companies the group does not exist at all. It consists of those whose responsibilities include all, or at least several of the traditional business functions. Its core consists of managers who have 'full profit responsibility'.

Next comes what I will call 'middle management', consisting of the managers who have other managers reporting to them, but excluding members of the two categories already defined.

Finally there is 'front-line management': managers (including foremen and supervisors) who directly control operative staff.

In any particular company, some of these categories may be missing, or they may be subdivided. But basically they are the four major categories recognized by the culture as a whole. Virtually every manager is aware of his category, just as most Englishmen are aware of their social class, and East African tribesmen know which 'age-set' they belong to. (Social and educational class and age are also important to managers. In Britain especially, but also in the U S, a graduate middle manager of 26 with class A B parents will be treated very differently from an academically unqualified middle manager of 45 from a working-class background. But these things are settled before the individual enters into management, and are virtually impossible to change thereafter. No question of rites of passage arises.)

Rites occur at each point of transition between the grades. A special set of rites marks the initial entry of the individual into management, whether such entry is by promotion, or by direct recruitment (of graduates, etc.) from outside. And, finally, the transfer of an individual from one company to another is invariably marked by ritual performances, whether or not the move is accompanied by a change of grade.

It is best to take as a first example the rites that surround the initial recruitment of individuals into the management culture. The initiation ritual includes most of the elements that make up the rituals at the various other transitions. There is an overall similarity. However, some of the elements are developed more ornately in the first ritual than at later stages. For at the initial stage management is taking the greatest gamble, and therefore needs most reassurance.

In most companies, the ritual of management recruitment is annual. The importance of recruiting graduates for management has been dinned home so often that very few companies feel happy unless they are gathering in their proportion of each years' crop. Like most aspects of management ritual, it first developed in the US, and has there reached its highest degree of dedication; but it has been religiously copied by British and other companies in their endless search to re-create by imitation the superior magic of the Americans. Even in industries with sufficient glamour (publishing, advertising, television) to ensure their being annually inundated with applications from graduates it is still considered necessary to advertise in the relevant publications.

In point of fact, most companies end up recruiting far more graduates than they know what to do with – one of the first indications that the whole process is a ritualistic rather than pragmatically useful one.[1]

1. This book was being prepared for the press when it was disclosed that in the UK graduate recruitment for management had fallen sharply off in 1971. This may be an acceleration of a trend I had already noticed, and discuss later. But the main factor is the prevailing economic climate. I would

So the ritual begins with advertisement, and the receipt of applications for membership. It moves on through the processes of selection. These vary widely from company to company, but common to all is the need to make up for two basic truths. They are unpleasant, and awareness of them is consciously repressed. For one, we do not know enough about the qualities that make an individual a successful manager (if indeed there are any particular ones) to define them. Secondly even if we did have that much knowledge, our psychological equipment is not adequate to discern them.

The search for 'potential managers' therefore assumes one or other of a variety of substitute processes. All of them are designed to eliminate those candidates who will be least acceptable to the managerial society. The first stage of the rite of passage is necessarily purificatory. Allegiance to the ideals of the previous, the academic, culture is one of the taints that will need to be removed. It obviously makes things simpler to choose candidates who appear to need the least purification. (This is neither a modern nor a transient phenomenon. The religions of academic life and management have always been almost polar opposites.)

Just as the first stage of the mystery rites of Eleusis in classical times was according to van Gennep to exclude 'those whose hands were impure and who spoke in an unintelligible fashion', the first stage of the recruitment ritual is to eliminate, via interview, application form and so on, candidates whose habits of behaviour and speech make them obviously unacceptable to the particular company concerned. In this respect, incidentally, the plummy, 'public school' accent may, even in England, be as great a handicap as the accents of Stepney, the Gorbals or the Bronx. Similarly, over-fashionable dress may be as unacceptable as sweater and jeans. Such individuality indicates a degree of commitment to the academic culture that will be impossible for the purificatory rites to wash out.

---

be surprised if recruitment did not pick up again once the economy expands once more. More important to my immediate point is the press coverage given to this disclosure. All the articles implied that somewhere something must have gone 'wrong'. Nobody suggested that what had happened was that management had come to its senses. I don't believe it myself.

Among the purificatory rites will be the process I mentioned in the Introduction, the meaningless taking of references. They will include the filling in of elaborate application forms with a preponderance of items totally irrelevant to any conceivable assessment of managerial capacity (height?, weight?, parents' nationality?, name of school?). Their ritual nature is self-evident to anyone who can look at them for a few moments with any degree of objectivity.

Yet to suggest the elimination of any such encrustations is to provoke hostile reactions (and not only from those whose livelihood depends on the compilation and recording of irrelevant detail). Either one is greeted with immediate indignation, or one is met by the kind of embarrassed silence reserved for those who publicly commit socially unpardonable offences. Both reactions are of course evidence of having touched on a sensitive spot.

Once selection is achieved, the next step in the ritual is to segregate the candidates for a while in a category labelled 'management trainees'. The period of segregation varies. It can be as short as three months, and as long as two years. An initial period of intensive indoctrination in the beliefs and ethics of management completes the stage of purification. The candidates then spend their time much as the novices among the Australian tribes, being instructed in tribal law and 'witnessing totem ceremonies, recitation of myths, etc.' The close of the period is marked with a variety of local rites, most of which have two elements in common. There is a ceremonial meeting with the chief executive and (sometimes or) his directorate, and a ritual meal (usually dinner, sometimes lunch) which the novices eat together with a selected group of their future colleagues.

The ceremonial meeting and the common meal are virtually universal means of manifesting the binding-together which is the kernel of the rite of incorporation. The common meal forms the basis of the central Christian sacrament. The importance of the 'staff canteen' in some companies' thinking is also a manifestation of this primal belief. In some cases novices take part in a series of such ritual meals. Thus links are forged gradually, rather than instantaneously. But even in

such cases, the end of the period of novitiate is usually marked
by a meal of special significance.

In recent years the practical uselessness of this whole procedure has become fairly evident. It has been more or less
abandoned in some companies. In particular the period of
limbo-like existence as a 'management trainee' has been dras-
tically shortened, and even eliminated. 'We only appoint to
specific jobs' has been part of the recruitment creed of some
such trail-blazing companies. One would be more impressed by
such a move were it to represent a change in reality rather
than in form. In fact, however, most of the 'specific jobs' turn
out to have been dreamed up solely for the purpose of accom-
modating new recruits rather than because of any intrinsic
need. As such they are normally readily indentifiable by other
members of the firm and by outsiders. The occupants of the
posts are still treated with that mixture of reserve, jealousy
and kindly tolerance which in more orthodox companies is
given to management trainees.

This phenomenon explains the recent sprouting of positions
with the title 'assistant to' some established manager. Organization theorists have tried hard to describe and justify the
difference between, for example, the 'Assistant to the Sales
Manager' and the 'Assistant Sales Manager'. None of the explanations match the facts of the situation: 'assistants to' are
people in the transitional stage of the initiation ritual, while
'assistants' are initiated members of the culture on their way
up the hierarchy.

For there exists a virtually universal rule. In crossing the
gap that separates one category of the hierarchy from another
the individual must spend some time assisting a member of the
superior category. Most of the rites of passage from one category to another, whatever the level, have much in common
with the initiation rites. In many cases, however, we find the
additional ritual of performance assessment.

In theory, performance assessment should be useful. Recording each year the objectives set for an individual and the degree to which he achieved them, and basing his promotion
prospects on that record, has a convincing logic about it. In
practice it doesn't work. Setting measurable objectives is a

highly complex matter, and so is measuring the individual's
success in achieving them. (Necessarily one has to allow for
the side-effects of other people's efforts and changes in the
environment.) Consequently the persons responsible either give
up, or substitute objectives which can be measured but have
little relation to the realistic needs of the business. At best such
systems become simply the recording of subjective estimates of
the manager by his superior. If the superiors are good enough,
this isn't a bad way of going about things. It does mean however that both good and bad managements tend to perpetuate
themselves, and is one reason why in business as in other walks
of life the rich get richer and the poor get poorer.

Once past the selection stage, the candidate for promotion
again faces a transitional period in which he is neither one
thing nor the other. Such a period used to be spent as an
assistant. Nowadays in most companies this is not enough to
satisfy the emotional demand for a period of seclusion. It is an
inevitable requirement of most contemporary rites that the
candidate spend at least some time, perhaps as little as a few
weeks, perhaps as much as a year, physically removed from
the company. This period normally is spent on a course, either
organized by the company and limited to its members, or
organized by some outside establishment. During such a
course, interestingly enough, the candidates are usually removed from many of the restraints that inhibit their behaviour
in the working environment. Such a relaxation of normal behavioural restrictions is a recurrent characteristic of the transitional stage of rites of passage in most parts of the world.

I am not denying that the member of a course learns much
that is useful, at least sometimes. The same is true of aboriginal initiation. And yet such courses are ritualistic in nature.
They normally terminate with the same kind of communal
meal and meeting that marks the end of the novice's initiation.
The magical attitude of most members of the culture towards
such courses is further underlined by the way in which the
individual is treated when he returns to his normal environment. It is rare that completion of the ritual is immediately
followed by reassignment. Even in those companies where the
directorate has bent over backwards to make it clear that selec-

tion for a course does not necessarily imply special favour, the
returned candidate is treated in a markedly different way from
the ordinary manager. His selection, and his new knowledge,
both set him apart as a 'man of power', and, as ever, his only
vaguely understood power is conceived as dangerous, and requires him to be treated with circumspection, if not necessarily respect. Frequently, this new feeling manifests itself
negatively, in teasing, denigration of 'book learning', even in
antagonism and insult, especially from members of his old
caste who would have considered themselves his superior (and
may indeed still be formally senior to him).

Normally, this is genuinely worrying to the candidate, even
though he will usually interpret it as opposition to new ideas
rather than an emotional antagonism to him personally. The
problem of post-course acculturation has preoccupied many of
the more enlightened organizers of training programmes. The
best that can probably be done is to forewarn the candidate of
the attitudes he is likely to meet, and prepare him for them.
They are manifestations of much too basic an emotion ever to
be fully removed.

In any case there are compensations. Members of the grade
to which he has just been initiated will join him in ritual acts
of eating and drinking designed to mark his incorporation, and
members of his own grade may noticeably imitate his behaviour, and associate with him in an attempt to attract good luck
by contagion. He will gradually be accorded other signs of
respect and recognition by staff members of all grades, until he
is actually given an appointment consonant with his new
status. By then he will be emotionally attuned to it. The necessity for such emotional attunement is of course one of the
major psychological reasons for the lengthy ritual.

Occasionally one comes across someone who has been trans-
lated from one grade to another without the necessary rituals
having taken place. In such cases I have invariably observed
signs of emotional distress. It shows itself typically in a period
of withdrawal accompanied by a vigorous attempt to assert
status by the accumulation of material symbols (a larger office,
an extra secretary, an assistant, a chauffeur). There followed a
period spent concentrating on eating ritual meals with his new

colleagues. At a high enough level, he is also likely to spend a great deal of time associating with the chief executive, and emphasizing the closeness of their relationship.

In the end assimilation usually takes place, but only after a long and rather painful period. It demonstrates that ritual, while pragmatically pointless, may well be psychologically necessary.

Such omission of ritual is most likely to occur when the change of grade is accompanied by a change of company. I see two reasons. On the one hand, the recipient company may well not be aware that a change of grade is involved. The marks of gradation (for instance, the title of director) vary considerably, so the new company may well assume that the individual concerned has already been initiated. Or, since the rites of incorporation may vary from company to company, the individual may not recognize them for what they are. A regular morning telephone call from the chief executive, which in the company at large may be recognized as a mark of incorporation into the directorate, may well be assumed by the stranger to be routine. Alienation is likely to occur if he looks for the symbols he would have expected in his own company, and fails to find them.

Usually classed among rites of passage are funerary rites – the rituals that accompany the departure of the individual. Such rites too have their equivalent in management. But they are important enough to warrant a special chapter to themselves.

8. Funerary Rites

Among the northern branch of the Ostyaks, a Siberian tribe, the spirits of the dead inhabit a land beyond the mouth of the river Ob, on the bed of the Arctic Ocean. The road that leads to that underwater world has three forks, leading to three separate entrances – one for sinners, one for those who have lived a blameless life, and one for those who have died of violence or suicide. The road is dark, and the journey long. When a man dies, his body is laid on a boat on the frozen ground with all the things he will need on his journey. His womenfolk make a doll, wash, dress and feed it each day of his journey. When he finally reaches the land of the dead, the doll is placed on his tomb.

Virtually all societies have believed in a life after death. For such societies, death is a transition, like birth and maturation. The rituals that surround it therefore take the form of rites of passage. First there is a rite of separation from the living (laying the body on the boat). It is followed by a period of transition (the journey north, while there is still a connection between the doll and the travelling spirit), and finally a rite of incorporation with the dead (the laying to rest of the doll).

However, the emotions that surround death are stronger than those attending other transitions, and the ritual has to reflect that difference. It also has to reflect the fact that those emotions are of three kinds whose relative importance varies from society to society: *bereavement,* the reaction to the loss of the dead person; *fear of death,* since an actual death is the most potent intimation of mortality; and *fear of the dead,* whether it is fear of the supernatural power of the dead, and conceivably vindictive spirit, or of the actual return of the dead man.

The rites must thus mark the separation of the individual from the living and his incorporation into the dead, express bereavement, and ensure that the dead spirit is placated, or at least prevented from returning. These elements can be traced in the funerary rites of our own society, both the formal ones of Christianity, and the informal ones of social custom.

Now managers rarely die in harness, and when they do the rites prescribed by the culture at large supersede any that may develop within management. But the same patterns of emotion, the same ritual idiom with which the primitive confronts the fact of death, appear uncannily paralleled in the rituals with which management surrounds its equivalent of death – retirement, resignation and dismissal.

It is no mere coincidence that three phenomena should be involved, and that the northward road of the Ostyaks should have three forks. Death can come naturally, as does retirement. It can come by one's own hand, as does resignation. Or it can come unnaturally through violence or accident, as does dismissal (including redundancy). In each case the emotional effect on the survivors is different, and demands a difference in the pattern of ritual that accompanies the event.

Differences also show between cultures in the degree of emotion that is displayed by the mourners and allowed for in the prescribed ritual. When an Australian aborigine dies in some tribes his skull is pounded to bits, and his legs broken so that he may not pursue the living. Among the Navaho the man's lodge is burned with everything in it. With the more placid Pueblo Indians excess of passion disappears – the man's hairbrush is broken, not his bones, and only his bow and arrow and his corn fetish are buried with him. A moderate display of grief replaces an orgy of terror, but the elements of the ritual remain essentially the same.

Similarly the intensity of emotion surrounding departure rituals varies from company to company, but the ritual elements remain the same everywhere.

Retirement is the expected and inevitable end to any manager's career, just as death is the inevitable end of every human being. It is reasonable therefore that both events should engender comparable emotions. According to Christian and many non-Christian traditions death is the prelude to unparalleled bliss, at least for those who have lived properly. A basic tenet of management beliefs too is that retirement is a happy time. And an important part of the rituals of the management society is that retirement must by convention be painted in envious terms.

To admit that one is afraid of retirement is an admission of failure, and, more importantly, a confession of misbehaviour, as well as a challenge to accepted dogma. In the same way, for a Christian to admit to the fear of death is either to deny an essential element of his faith, or to admit to unpardonable sin.

The subject therefore is taboo. The very intensity of the taboo is an indication that the dogma about retirement is a false pretence. Managers fear retirement and the consequent feelings of exclusion, rejection and uselessness, as much as men fear biological death – on occasion perhaps even more so. That is why they must pretend to the world and themselves that they don't.

Thus an essential part of the ritual that surrounds the event of retirement is the reassurance of the individual concerned. Every person he meets will formally congratulate him on his impending departure. The congratulations reach their height at the party, lunch, dinner, reception or other formal gathering with which the ritual culminates.

The congratulations, the expressions of envy and admiration, in fact have two separate motives, both of which are perceptible in the funeral rites of nearly all societies. One is the reassurance of the survivors. Reminded by the event of the inevitability of their own retirement, they need to express their faith that it is not to be feared. The other motive is the placation of the departing manager. While, objectively, no one could be more harmless than a retiring manager, superstitious fear makes it necessary to ensure that he is contented and bears no grudges. He is therefore praised, his major feats are recounted, and the ceremony culminates with a speech in which the departing manager, whatever the truth of the situation, affirms the happiness of the years he has spent with the company. Gifts are almost invariably inscribed with some formula that emphasizes the termination of his connection with the company. In some companies the ritual also includes reassurance that he will be 'kept in touch' – the implication being that of the theatrical agent's traditional 'don't ring us, we'll ring you'.

A transitional period ensues during which all traces of his presence are eliminated, his office cleared, his personal possessions returned to him or destroyed, until nothing is left that might tempt him to return. In all this his secretary has a particularly important role to play, as the person most qualified to carry out the purification rites. That over, in a very few companies she is required (by convention if not by law) to leave too, as the Hindu widow is expected to immolate herself on her husband's pyre. Almost universally she is transferred to another department, rather than being allowed to continue working for her boss's successor. (It is very likely that she herself would feel this to be wrong.) She is much too powerful a link with the retired man's spirit to be allowed to remain.

Once purification is complete, the final act of the ritual involves the dispatch of an emissary, usually a close colleague, to visit the retired individual, and ensure that he is 'settling down'. Overtly, such a visit is an expression of sympathy (though if retirement is an enviable state, why should sympathy be necessary?) In fact it represents the final laying to rest of the ghost: reassurance for the survivors that the wandering spirit has finally reached the land of the dead.

In the vast majority of companies, however, contact with the retired manager continues through the regular payment of a pension. The motives may be mixed (there is certainly an expiatory element), but part of the purpose is undoubtedly continued placation, just as in many tribes regular ritual sacrifices to the spirits of the dead, usually one's ancestors, are necessary to avoid their displeasure or even return.

More obviously ritualistic are further measures that some companies take to ensure the same ends – sending the house journal, or even special regular newsletters, organizing annual reunion lunches, dinners or garden-parties. The desire of the retired to return is considered so strong in such companies that unless it is given the opportunity for ritual expression it will manifest itself in more unpleasant ways – in the extreme by an actual return to the work-place. I have never seen this happen, but have heard reports of it. It is an occasion of acute emotional stress.

Much the same pattern of ritual surrounds the process of resignation before retiring age, though the motivations vary considerably. Technically, resignation equates with suicide. On the other hand it is a genuinely envied state, since normally it is a precursor of transition up the hierarchy. It is difficult therefore for a Western mind to appreciate the parallel, but links can be found with the attitude to suicide in those few cultures where it is seen not only as a proper act, but as a preliminary to favoured existence in the after-life.

The expressions of congratulation and envy which convention demands be paid to the resigner are more likely to be genuinely felt, and less blatantly ritualistic. For that very reason, it is permissible, though it doesn't happen often, to express disapproval. To say to someone resigning 'I think you're making a mistake' is allowable, to tell someone who is retiring 'You'll hate every moment' is almost inconceivable, and unforgivable.

The ceremonials tend to be less elaborate and expensive. There is less need to reassure and protect the survivors. Presentation gifts are much less likely to be inscribed, and what inscriptions there are will probably emphasize past companionship rather than the fact of separation. For the resigner is about to increase his power. The occasion is seized to remind the departing individual of services done to him and debts he owes (whereas the retiring manager will be reminded of the things he has done, and the debts owed to him). For the person retiring, accepted phraseology is likely to be something like: 'Forget those income tax forms – I think we can let you off those now.' For the resigner it is more likely to be: 'Don't forget – I'm still relying on you for those tax returns.'

Mementoes of his presence are allowed to remain, and are even deliberately kept. His secretary, unless he takes her with him, is likely to remain in the same place, and to continue working for his successor. Every effort will be made to ensure that the good luck he has displayed rubs off on the survivors. Contagion for once is sought rather than shunned.

There is no need for the elaborate precautions against return that are taken for the retired. There may be a ritual visit to him in his new environment, but no one will be unduly worried if it doesn't take place. Usually he will not be invited to reunions, nor will he be sent house journals or letters. Since his re-appearance is not a danger, there is no need to guard against it, or provide formal opportunities for restricting it.

At least this is true of the colleagues and associates of the resigner. It may not be true of the official attitude of the direc-torate, the resigner's superior, or the personnel department. For each of them a resignation may well be an uncomfortable event, either as a direct criticism or as an omen of future misfortune. As a counter-charm many companies have de-veloped a small piece of ritual called the 'leaving interview'. Sometimes this is a simple affair between the man and his boss. Ever more frequently it is an elaborate event involving special-ists from the personnel department, and organized by them. In either case it has the same complex purpose.

The occasion serves to place on record the resigner's reasons for leaving. Overtly this may be its only purpose, but if there really were no other reason there would be no call for elabora-tion. A written note would do. But the interview is normally held even where a resignation letter has been written. For the main purpose of the interview is to assert with the force of ritual that the company is sorry to see the man go, is grateful for his efforts in the past, and wishes him nothing but success in the future. None of these things need be true, but it is import-ant that the person leaving accepts them. Otherwise he may be resentful, and a resentful spirit, in the philosophy of such companies is a dangerous one, even though it may not be very clear exactly what harm he would be capable of.

The interview has a further purpose: the reassurance that the departure is not an ill omen. Sniffing out such omens is the major reason why specialist witch-doctors are called in to such sessions. Their medicine is supposed to tell whether the resig-nation will be followed by others, whether it is a symptom of generally low morale, or whether it is simply what it seems to be to the layman.

The witch-doctor himself is in a rather difficult position. If he sniffs out some evil influence he lays himself and his col-leagues open to criticism, as their medicine had no success in keeping such evil spirits ('poor morale', 'bad organization', 'frustration', 'demotivation') away. If he invariably gives a clean bill of health, however, he will soon find his usefulness questioned.

From time to time, therefore, the witch-doctor will decide that more lies behind the resignation than meets the eye. This provides a signal for any one of several purificatory rites that are used by different schools of thought. The most common is a series of rites designed to drive out 'bad communication' (the most frequently diagnosed cause of a surplus of resignations). They will include the setting up of liaison committees, founding, brightening-up or relaunching the house journal, organizing visits for the chief executive and his directorate, and a flurry of repetitions of such comforting incantatory proverbs as 'communication is two-way', 'communicate up, down, and sideways', 'communication is everyone's job'. During all this of course the witch-doctor will have to be careful to avoid the summoning of an outside rival as a consultant.

I have talked of the rituals accompanying retirement and resignation. Which leaves us with the question of dismissals, including both redundancy and involuntary resignation. Dismissals, like violent deaths, occur for a great variety of reasons, and the number of differing rituals is almost as large – certainly too great to go through in detail. However, here again certain rules are visible which always hold whatever the specific circumstances.

In the first place, an overt dismissal for misconduct or incompetence risks attracting the attention of the supernatural powers I talked about in Chapter 2. The higher the hierarchical grade involved, the more this applies. To lessen this fear, convention demands that, particularly near the top of the hierarchy, every pretence should be made that it is not a dismissal, but a resignation, or if possible an early retirement. Outwardly the rituals that are performed will be the same as those discussed above. On closer inspection, however, there will be significant differences.

For the second rule about all dismissals is that the fear of contagion is much greater than with any other kind of departure. This puts most members of the company in an ambivalent position which can cause some stress. For while the fear of contagious ill-luck leads to a desire to shun the unfortunate individual, the requirement to placate him demands some form of contact in order to express sympathy, and if possible, to convince him that it is all for the best, really. One effect of this is that the dismissed individual can expect letters and phone-calls of condolence, rather than face-to-face meetings: exactly the opposite is true for the resigner. Where he himself causes a meeting, he can expect an effusive welcome. But he will also notice nervous glances and all the other behavioural traits by which we exhibit an unfocused fear.

There is unlikely to be any formal gathering to mark the dismissal, though friends will express their genuine sympathy and sorrow at an informal gathering, in a ritual with no in-strumental connotations. In place of the formal gathering, the accepted ritual for a dismissal, even when cast as a feigned resignation, will be an exchange of letters to lend the magical authority of a written document to the pretence of retirement or resignation. It is also a device to avoid the possible con-tagion of a face-to-face meeting.

With dismissal the transition period after separation is longer and more danger-ridden than any other kind of de-parture. It consists of two stages.

The period from the exchange of letters until he actually leaves the company is usually made as short as possible. It may be extended, especially where the manager is a member of the directorate. I know of one director who remained with his company, in a different building admittedly, for six months after it was generally known that his 'resignation' had been accepted. It was not made public until a blaze of publicity fol-lowing the voluntary resignation of one or two other senior executives gave an opportunity for announcing it without in-creasing the amount of attention the company was getting. During the six months of his unnatural stay, other staff in the building grew used to referring to him as 'the ghost'. It was one of the incidents that helped create the idea for this book.

The second stage of transition lasts from the time he actu-ally leaves until he starts a new job and is ritually incorporated into the new company. During this period the dismissed man-ager is at his most dangerous as a source of contagion, as he will find out if he returns to his former office. The situation is worse if he has been made redundant, since there is then no reason to blame him for his misfortune: bad luck is more to be feared than incompetence or villainy, since there is no protection against it.

Occasionally a departure will take place in confused circumstances that make it difficult to classify it as a dismissal or a resignation. This occurs in particular after a political clash within the company, when the losers may be as eager to leave as the winners are to see them go. It happened after the Reed-I P C merger, and more than once in the short and stormy history of London Weekend Television. Those who left had a large number of sympathizers among the survivors. The rites of departure, at least at I P C, but, from what I hear, at L W T too, were transformed into occasions for unnatural gaiety, as individuals seized the opportunity ritually to emphasize and express their sense of community, suppressing in the excitement their fear of contagion.

Even in such cases, however, the pattern of the rite of passage is visible. In the transitional period the individual concerned is a source of danger to be handled in ritually prescribed ways, or not at all. In a word, he is *taboo*. Which is the subject of the next chapter.

9. Taboos

Many years ago in a tobacco factory in England, one of the labourers whose job it was to keep the cigarette machines stocked with supplies of tobacco discovered that, by the simple expedient of replenishing all the machines at the same time instead of waiting till they ran out, he could cut his working time to about five minutes in every twenty. For the remaining fifteen he went off to the rest room to smoke, read the papers, and do crossword puzzles. It was about half a day before his behaviour, which had if anything improved the productivity of the section, was reported. He was summoned before the foreman, forced to repent, and made to promise that he would return to the established work pattern.

Much more recently, in the London headquarters of a major public company, an accountant working on 'profit planning' spent some time with one of the company's acknowledgedly 'creative' groups. Among its other pastimes, this group was given to playing chess in normal working hours. Most of its productive work was necessarily done in emergency sessions which involved overnight or weekend working. A keen chess player himself, he started dropping in for a game at lunchtime or in his own moments of enforced idleness. It was only a few days before he was carpeted by his boss and ordered to stop it. For his own good.

The appearance of idleness must be avoided, whatever the reality of the situation. The labourer has learned that for him the rest room is a forbidden place except at the ritually prescribed times. The accountant has understood that, except when ritually necessary, he must not come into contact with 'creative' people.

The universe of the manager is full of such proscriptions – of places he may not enter, people he may not associate with, things he must not do. So is the world of the primitive. And the word that is normally used to label this particular kind of ritual proscription is 'taboo'.

Since Captain Cook borrowed the word from the Tongans in 1774 to describe their society, it has found a place in virtually every civilized language, both as a technical anthropological term and as a colloquialism. The speed and extent of the spread are evidence of the universality of the phenomenon.

Primarily, the adjective 'taboo' is applied to a person, a place or a thing with which contact is dangerous. To apply it to types of behaviour is a slight distortion of the original meaning, but there are enough precedents to justify it. The underlying emotional attitude is the same. What we feel on observing someone act in a taboo way is exactly what we feel on seeing him touch a taboo object or enter a taboo place.

Taboo usually signifies 'supernatural' danger. But, as I have pointed out, it is not always easy to distinguish between natural and supernatural. For many societies the difference does not exist at all. If a savage shuns the company of someone who is recently bereaved, the affected person is in a taboo state. On the other hand, when we ourselves refuse to associate with someone with smallpox, we consider this a rational act, not the observance of a taboo. But how should one classify the act of a savage who, knowing nothing about viruses, shuns a smallpox victim? Or our own behaviour in avoiding the company of people suffering from psychological disturbances? It is tempting to assert that avoidance of this kind is rational when we understand the mechanism of contagion, and irrational, and therefore to be called 'taboo', when we don't.

But this is an arrogant and unhelpful attitude. The savage is in no doubt that he (or at least the wise men of his tribe) 'understands' the mechanism of contagion, just as we believe ourselves (or at least our doctors) to understand the spread of viruses. For my own purposes therefore I will be using 'taboo' in connection with any avoidance reaction where the danger is anything but tangible, immediate, and overt. This is not entirely watertight itself. But it does allow me to distinguish between avoiding Central Park after dark, which is not observing a taboo, and the kind of behaviour I described earlier, which is, even if it is possible to advance 'rational' reasons for it.

In any case it is rational to avoid a danger one believes in, whether or not the belief is true. What distinguishes scientific from magico-religious behaviour are the tests that one carries out to determine the objective validity of the belief. Most of the managerial beliefs I will be dealing with in this chapter are considered self-evident and beyond the need for testing. That puts them necessarily in the realm of magic and religion.

Sometimes, indeed, the fear the manager exhibits is much less well-defined than that of the primitive. The Australian aborigine is clear about what will happen if he breaks taboo, by, say, eating the flesh of his totem at other than a ritually approved time: he will turn grey, suffer from ophthalmia and skin eruptions, and perhaps die. But the foreman and the chief accountant who were so concerned that their subordinates should not break the taboo against idleness were in no such clear-cut position.

In neither case was there any question of the work of their department suffering as a result; nor was there any chance of the behaviour really being noticed by anyone in higher authority. What was motivating both of them was a certainty born of conditioning and education that such behaviour was simply wrong, and that it invited retribution, though from where is undefined.

Retribution of course may well fall on the sinner and his associates alike, which is why the manager is so concerned to ensure that his subordinates observe taboo as rigorously as he does, and why he is likely to be alarmed at the knowledge that his superiors or colleagues have broken it. That breach of taboo endangers not only the individual but also his community is a virtually universal belief.

All four kinds of taboo – persons, places, things and behaviour – are manifestly present in managerial society. There are sufficient differences to make it worth treating each separately. Since the most widespread examples concern persons it seems best to start with them.

It is essential to realize that the avoidance response of taboo is the same whether the person concerned is viewed as evil or as good. Taboo is not the same as sending to Coventry. It is in no wise a punishment inflicted on the taboo person. Frequently the primitive tribe makes neither a linguistic nor a behavioural distinction between the 'unclean' or the 'sacred'. Kings, priests, pregnant or menstruating women, infants, murderers and people struck by lightning, are all, according to the culture, likely to be considered taboo. Anyone who is markedly different, whether permanently or temporarily, will tend to be taboo, as will strangers or people whose actions are not understood.

But the strongest taboos of all are those that surround the chief executive, and particularly the owner-manager. He is ritually speaking the most powerful and therefore, irrespective of his personal character, the most dangerous – even where the actual personal power he can wield is minimal. A manager may even be openly scornful of the power of the chief executive, either because he is secure in his own position or is a member of the entourage of one of the divisional heads whose pragmatic power is often greater than their nominal chief's. But that same manager will avoid as far as possible the presence of the despised boss, except on ritually approved occasions. If circumstances should force contact upon him, his behaviour will change markedly. He will observe all the normal behavioural taboos with much more rigour than usual, attempt the maximum neutrality, seek the background, and in general exhibit the behaviour of someone who is trying not to attract attention.

The attempt to avoid attention is a common feature of the behaviour associated with taboo. In our particular case the caution is not designed to avoid the attention of the chief executive himself. For the fear is not of the man, but of the power he symbolizes and the forces that surround him because of his position. It is these invisible forces that must not be aroused.

Anyone who has recently been the victim of misfortune is normally treated in the same way, at least until it becomes manifest that his spell of bad luck has ended. Too, the power-taboo that shrouds the chief executive is evident, to a lesser degree, in his chief lieutenants: indeed to some extent any superior manager is taboo to his subordinates.

The second major category of taboo persons consists of outsiders. The degree to which their contact is feared varies naturally according to the power they are believed to wield, or at least be in contact with. The journalist, with his special relationship to the supernatural force of public opinion, is stringently taboo. In most cases, nobody is allowed near him except those who command special medicine themselves. Even the power of the chief executive is usually considered an insufficient safeguard against harm. He is only allowed to meet the journalist with the advice and in the presence of a P R man (one of the sorcerers I discussed in Chapter 4). The rituals and charms by which companies, on the advice of their P R men, guard against the dangers of the Press are numerous. As a rite of incorporation, the symbolic meal is virtually universal. Here it is an attempt to incorporate the stranger into the tribe, as well as an attempt to placate him and any powers there may be about him. Rarely, however, is it allowed to stand on its own. Even afterwards the P R man will still be cautiously on guard with whatever counter-magic he favours. Rarely too will there be present at the actual meal anyone whose own intrinsic powers are not considerable: the chief executive, his expert advisers, perhaps his divisional chiefs. For the eating of a meal is, invariably, a time of special danger. Only the strong can take the risk.

Much the same rituals apply to the arrival of any other outsider. One group worthy of special mention however are the auditors, whose religious power is such that no one is normally allowed to approach them except the company's own priests. Particular precautions are taken to ensure that the auditors do not meet unanointed members of the company at meals. I have known at least one company take this so far as to set aside a special office as a temporary canteen.

The exalted, the unfortunate and the strange are the major categories of taboo persons. But the system does not end there. In fact, as in many primitive cultures, everyone is taboo to someone. Almost everywhere white and blue collar workers are mutually taboo; so too are the various grades of the hierarchy I described in the last chapter. Mingling between them is very rarely proscribed by law, but normally stopped by a general feeling that it is both wrong and dangerous: a tempting of Providence. Even the companies that boast of their 'demo-cratic' canteen arrangements tend to do so defiantly, with much the same air as an atheistic Jew cooking steaks in butter. There would be no call to boast about it if it was not felt to be a dangerous act.

Occupations are also often mutually taboo. It is not surpris-ing that accountants, in view of their priestly status, avoid contact with other people (and are avoided by them). But much the same caution is true of creative groups of various kinds, engineers, salesmen, and 'admin' people. They avoid contact because it is believed to weaken their individual powers.

This necessity to keep apart categories of people who are mutually taboo is a major component of most place taboos in the management culture. The situation in one London news-paper building (not I P C) is typical of what happens in most companies.

The front lobby is taboo to all production staff. Since how-ever members of the public are allowed, indeed invited, in, the taboo only applies to the production staff in their working role. If they remove the symbols of that role – overalls of various kinds – the taboo vanishes.

One floor of the building is taboo to all except the director-ate, and one or two members of each department who are specially empowered to act as go-betweens. Whenever these go-betweens are summoned to the floor in question their behavi-our changes. They become nervous and, interestingly from a ritual point of view, tend to wash their hands and faces and use the lavatories. In view of the irregular timing of such sum-monses, this act can have only ritual purificatory significance.

Each section of the production floors is taboo to anyone who works in a different section – except again for a few specially empowered individuals. Thus the picture editor is allowed in the process department and the telephoto room. The printer's deputy – not the printer himself, except in emergency – and one or two particular stonehands are allowed into the editorial rooms; and so on. The taboos, surprisingly perhaps, extend to the directorate.

The only exempt personnel are the messengers (who are men past ambition rather than boys) and the cleaners, who in this respect fill much the same role as the Untouchable caste in Hindu society.

Two things are of general importance about this particular taboo-structure. One is that the taboos apply even when the departments are empty. Though they may have had their genesis in the need to keep apart groups of people who are taboo, they now indicate the existence of a more sophisticated set of beliefs – that the power which resides in or is associated with individuals can 'rub off' on to their surroundings. Secondly, none of these practices are the result of managerial (or union) prohibitions. They are all examples of behaviour patterns that have evolved to meet a universal feeling that to behave otherwise would be wrong.

In the management culture taboo objects, like taboo places, tend to be dangerous as a result of their association with taboo persons. I know of no equivalent in management to the holy objects of many religions, which are taboo because of their own intrinsic virtue or evil. Charms and fetishes are plentiful – an office is hardly complete without wall-chart, graph or some symbolic reminder of past successes – but on the whole they are not considered dangerous. Though powerful, they are not taboo.

The only taboo objects therefore are those which become dangerous through association with a taboo person. The office furniture, files and personal impedimenta of a dismissed manager for instance must be destroyed or cleaned before they are used again. And if they are used again it will not be by the dismissed man's successors, nor will it be while the dismissed man is still in the transitional period. Nothing like the same care is taken with the effects of someone who has genuinely resigned. There may even be a scramble for them among people trying to attract luck to themselves.

This phenomenon reaches a peak with the effects of a chief executive. If he has been dismissed they will be disposed of completely. If he has died or retired honourably, they may even form the nucleus of a shrine, though the more common method of commemoration is the display of a portrait.

There are four major classes of behaviour which are tabooed throughout the management culture. I have yet to find a company in which none of these prohibitions exist. Sometimes the restrictions may contribute to the company's success; often they are patently harmful; most of the time they are irrelevant.

The first major category forbids any kind of behaviour that marks out the individual as special, or attracts attention. The underlying fear is obvious: the attention that is attracted may be that of a malevolent or jealous spirit. Ruled out for instance are abnormalities of speech or dress (to be too well-dressed is as bad as to be careless); extreme parsimony or extreme generosity; odd eating or drinking habits; never to take holidays, or to take them in odd places; a liking for unusual working hours. To be safe – and for others to be safe around him – the manager must be conspicuously inconspicuous. Like the Buddhist following the Eightfold Path, he must be moderate in all things.

Forbidden therefore are exceptionally brilliant and exceptionally poor performance. A former colleague of mine labelled the reason for this phenomenon the Principle of Maximum Mediocrity. (Since to invent such a principle is itself egregious behaviour, I am withholding his name.) The principle manifests itself mainly when a job vacancy is to be filled. Neither the brilliant nor the poor candidates will be accepted. Instead the position will go to the most mediocre. The others are too dangerous.

The manager must also be modest in his patterns of consumption. Or, to be accurate, he must stick to the pattern that suits his station. I remember the shocked look on one manager's face when I told him I had arranged for a seminar for middle managers to be held at the Royal Garden Hotel. 'But that's where the directors go!' he protested. There must have been a similarly shocked look on the face of some managers in another company who insisted that a friend of mine pay his own bill for staying at the Savoy instead of a hotel more suitable to his station. The Savoy was no more expensive than hotels he had previously stayed in, and it was closer to his office. But it sounded too grand.

Another friend of mine got a similar reaction when he bought a house in the same road as his managing director, about three hierarchical grades above him. At a different level in a different company, there was considerable concern when the members of one department clubbed together to acquire an old refrigerator, installed it in their open-plan office, and stocked it with beer and champagne (of no particular distinction in defence against a sticky London summer. The point isn't that the company's money is being spent. The reaction is equally intense when it is the manager's own money, as it was in the last two instances. The point is that living above one's station (or markedly below it) attracts attention, and the risk of misfortune.

The second widespread behavioural taboo is doing or saying anything that 'rocks the boat'. Dissension threatens the peace and endangers the 'team-spirit' that every company is supposed to be proud of. Listen to any manager, in any company, anywhere in the management culture, who has something critical to say at a meeting. 'That's not a bad idea – particularly that bit about . . . But I can't quite agree . . .' The idiom varies, but the pattern remains the same. The manager has learnt that criticism must always be preceded by compliment.

It is interesting to note how common this taboo is in primitive cultures. The Tallensi of Ghana for instance believed that their land would not prosper unless everyone was at peace at the time of the public religious festivals. The ancient Greeks felt much the same way about the time of the Olympic Games. In *Patterns of Culture*, Ruth Benedict describes the council of the Zuni Indians and produces a picture that could be of an ideal Board of Directors: 'Since priests are holy men and must never during the prosecution of their duties feel anger, nothing is brought before them about which there will not be unanimous agreement.' And when the Karimojong of East Africa assemble for their succession ritual 'no one must make a noise, still less fight; no one must steal, no one must rake up old disputes by asking for the repayment of debts; no one must even beg from another' (Lucy Mair: *Primitive Government*).

Open dissension and genuine argument, even the clash of opposed personalities, are healthier than the same things suppressed and driven underground. They may even be fruitful. But they introduce eddies and whirlpools into the comforting flow of events. They stand out from the safe grey background.

Such things are dangerous. They are therefore taboo in the management culture.

I have already touched upon the third major taboo area. It is the general prohibition against being (or rather appearing) idle. This happens to be one of the few examples of a direct clash between management science and management magic. For it is fairly easy to prove with the techniques of Queueing Theory that if the arrival of tasks and the length of time needed to carry them out are random then either there must always be idle resources, or the tasks will tend to form an 'Infinite Queue'. In anything except a purely routine management situation, either there are idle people around all the time – they needn't always be the same people – or the whole place will seize up eventually.

In a few places, notably the editorial departments of newspapers, this truth had been recognized long before Queueing Theory was invented. Elsewhere it is very difficult to get managers to see the point, unless they have enough mathematics to appreciate the proof. In the managerial philosophy being idle is wrong, appearing to be idle is blatant sinning. It cries out for retribution. And any mathematical theory that says it is necessary is either a hoax or devil's work.

Just so did the sixteenth and seventeenth century Church react to Copernicus, Kepler and Galileo. And while the management hierarchy lacks the power to send people to the stake, it has enough power to make life unpleasant for anyone heretical enough to attempt to implement this particular conclusion of modern mathematics.

The last of the major taboo areas is perhaps the most emotional one of all. It concerns the prohibition that is almost universally laid on irreverence, that is, not taking one's job, or management, or business in general, seriously. How seriously this particular taboo is taken may be seen in the fact that it is nowhere legislated against. Most of the taboos I have so far mentioned will occasionally be found in written company regulations, or even in union-management agreements. But levity, as a reaction to the managerial environment, is such a heinous breach of taboo that it cannot be thought of, let alone be written about. For much the same reason, it will frequently go unpunished, at least directly. Breaking other taboos may lead to a carpeting, a reprimand, even on occasion the sack (though repentance is normally a safeguard against that). Laughing about the company, making jokes about the chairman, being sarcastic about the purpose of business, irreverently satirizing the seriousness of management are moral derelictions of such an order that they can only be ignored.

On the other hand, anyone given to this kind of behaviour will soon find that he himself has become taboo. He is much too dangerous an individual to be around.

To sum up the matter of behavioural taboos, let me again quote Ruth Benedict. She is describing the kind of man held in high regard among the Zuni, but you may recognize an ideal manager. 'The highest praise, describing an impeccable townsman, runs: "He is a nice polite man. No one ever hears anything from him. He never gets into trouble. He's Badger clan and Muhekwe kiva, and he always dances in the summer dances." He should "talk lots", as they say – that is he should always set people at their ease – and he should without fail cooperate easily with others either in the field or in ritual, never betraying a suspicion of arrogance or a strong emotion.'

A man who observes all the taboos is a highly-regarded manager and will undoubtedly reach high office, although he will not actively seek it. But if we relied on him for industrial progress, innovation, expansion, or whatever you like to call success, we would be in a backwater. Success demands excellence, which is an abnormal, egregious, attention-getting quality. Success therefore demands a breach of taboo.

Perhaps surprisingly, the management culture recognizes this. And the way it manages to have its cake and eat it is to postulate that there are individuals endowed with enough magical power of their own to challenge the supernatural forces and defeat them. Such men are the heroes, the kings, the demi-gods of the culture. About them I will have something to say later.

10. Sexual Taboos

It is not surprising that the most powerful of taboo structures, in any society, governs the relationships between men and women. How far the differences between the two are congenital, and how far they are created by society is immaterial. Social customs act to reinforce and exaggerate basic biological differences until the gulf that separates the two sexes becomes the greatest and most puzzling of all human barriers.

Our Western culture, though it may be moving in a more rational direction, is no exception to this rule. Neither is the management culture. But while the one is embedded in the other it frequently shows major differences. In the area of sex it does so by manifesting even stronger distinctions between the sexes, and an even stronger set of behavioural taboos.

It is not always easy to see, since outside taboos intrude into management more in this area than in any other, but generally the relationships between the sexes are much more stringently governed in business than they are outside. Half a century or so ago, the opposite was true. Management society was more permissive than the outside. But while the rest of the world has changed, management has been conservative.

One result is that most fictional attempts to describe sexual relationships in business fall flat. The novelist or scriptwriter projects his own, outside, standards and attitudes into the management world, and they simply do not fit.

My criticism is not that such novels, plays or films contain too much sex. Nor do I want to suggest that managers lead abnormally puritanical lives. What I am asserting is that they do not, like the heroes of some recent fiction, statutorily commit adultery with each new secretary that comes their way. In fact they behave in an extremely constrained manner in dealing with women in the management setting. Moreover, if a manager does have an affair with his secretary or any other close business contact, then he and his colleagues will react differently from the calm acceptance (or passionate emotion) normal in fiction. Everyone concerned will behave as if a taboo has been broken.

It would be unfair to single out particular examples for criticism. Instead I can present two favourable examples which display a more correct attitude. One is, perhaps oddly, in the James Bond series of thrillers. Bond is hardly a puritanical figure. But in Bond's relationship with Miss Moneypenny, with desire inhibited by a vague fear of transgression against an unspecified law, Ian Fleming is depicting very much the sense of taboo that affects managers.

Again, the B B C in its 'Brett' television series was realistic in giving its hero a mistress kept well apart from his workaday environment, even though she was known socially to his close colleagues. The writers were also correct in allowing him to invest in her gallery, while keeping it financially separate from his major holdings. The point is that even for a heroic figure like Brett, sexual entanglement within the management setting is felt to be dangerous. Any fictional affair in which allowance is not made for this feeling will never seem realistic, even if the reader cannot put his finger on the exact reason.

Another result of the conservatism of sexual attitudes in management is that the campaigns for equal pay or equal opportunity for women never get anywhere. Based on reasoned thinking, and again on the assumption that management philosophy has moved in step with outside beliefs, such campaigns miss the point: that the prohibitions and restrictions applied to women in the managerial society are the result of magico-religious beliefs. No amount of intellectual conviction will lead to their alteration.

For instance, it is true that women have more readily won acceptance in publishing, at least on the editorial side, than in most branches of industry. But two points need to be noticed.

By and large women are restricted to the feminine interest areas, which is an example of the taboo-system working in reverse. Not only women but women's affairs are taboo to men. Similarly, one of the few managerial ladders open to women in industry generally is in the personnel departments of companies with large female staffs, where the one specially sanctified woman provides a shelter against contact with others.

The second point is that where women have broken through into more general areas of newspaper work, as they have been doing more and more in the last twenty years, they have only done so at the expense of adopting masculine attributes. If they have not done so consciously, masculinity is attributed to them by their colleagues. It is a universal practice among the male members of editorial staffs (in private) to decry the sexual attractiveness of their colleagues. But not, be it noted, that of secretaries or the staff of other departments or, occasionally, women employed by other newspapers. Much the same pattern of behaviour is visible in other industries where women have succeeded in reaching managerial positions.

It is obviously a fear reaction. Since the derogatory comments are made irrespectively of the sexual appeal of the women concerned, they can only be ritual.

Whether or not one accepts increasing permissiveness as a mark of progress, it is undeniably true that, in the matter of sex, the management culture is much closer in its beliefs to most of the societies that we would normally label 'primitive' than it is to Western culture at large. For the essential fear in both cases is that except in certain approved ways contact with women will lessen a man's virility. Not in the usual contemporary sense of his sexual potency, but in the original sense of 'manliness' – the possession of qualities on which his success and prosperity depend.

For the savage, these qualities include physical strength and skill and prowess in hunting and fighting. For the manager it is a question rather of mental powers and clear reasoning, decision-making ability and prowess at profit-making. In each culture these are considered attributes in which women are deficient, partly for biological reasons, partly because they have a 'wrong' sense of values.

If a Bantu woman stepped over a sleeping man's legs, he believed he would not be able to run. Among the North American Indians contact with women was forbidden before joining a war party. On the Pacific Islands abstinence is necessary before a fishing expedition. The most dangerous form of contact is, not surprisingly, sexual intercourse, but any kind of contact is considered a threat, especially if the woman is pregnant or menstruating, when her sexual strangeness is at its height. The Pueblo Indians believe that touching a woman at these times will make a man ill. In 1873 the Journal of the Anthropological Institute reported a characteristic incident. An Australian aborigine who discovered that his wife had lain on his blanket during menstruation was so terrified that he killed her and died himself in a fortnight.

Places, objects and even activities associated with women are feared as well. The Khyoungthas of South-East India have a legend of a hero who won a kingdom by persuading the king and his followers to dress as women and perform female duties. They became so enfeebled they were conquered without a blow being struck.

Management mythology has no parallel tale to tell of a company which has gone under because its managers behaved effeminately. But tales abound of the impossibility of working properly under women executives. And the British publishing industry is convinced that at least one house failed because of the ascendancy the chairman's wife gained over him and the affairs of the business.

According to the stereotype, women are moody, changeable and unreliable (partly because of the menstrual cycle). They are insufficiently single-minded, readily distracted by other goals than making profits, and garrulous. They are emotional and only too ready to lose their tempers and create dissension. They are held to be also whimsical, arbitrary and unpredictable.

Such qualities are directly opposite to those supposed to make a good manager. Where the stereotype is believed to be true the surprise therefore is not that few women are accepted into the management hierarchy, but that any are at all. For some are – though not with the frequency or freedom that women nowadays become doctors or lawyers or administrative civil servants. And it is in its reaction to the exceptional few that the magical nature of the managerial attitude becomes most obvious.

For if one believes that women are as the stereotype says, it is a rational step not to make them managers. But even where a woman has been appointed a manager, thus demonstrating that she does not fit the stereotype, she is still taboo.

One significant manifestation of the taboo is the reluctance shown if someone suggests a woman member be appointed to a management committee or working party. Now committees are anyway viewed as a rather effeminate way of getting things done. We condemn a sterile committee as 'a Mothers' Union', or 'a lot of clucking hens', even though it may be more reminiscent of a gathering of crowing cocks. The virile manager despises them, and the closest parallel to the Khyoungtha myth I quoted earlier are probably the tales of companies that strangled themselves with committee procedure.

The physical presence of a woman increases still further the risk of impotence, which must be ritually averted. A woman will therefore be treated with exaggerated, almost caricatured, politeness. She is very likely to find empty seats on either side of her. Where there are only as many seats as people, these will be the last to be filled. Excessive regard will be paid to her comfort, and superficially at least to anything she says. She is very unlikely to be contradicted. If she leaves the room, there will be a general relaxation of tension. Almost invariably the next comment will be a joking one, though it need not necessarily be about the woman, or have sexual overtones at all.

All these are the reactions of taboo systems. They are the behaviour we exhibit towards something we do not understand and are afraid of – even down to the need to joke to indicate that the danger has passed.

The same reaction can be observed at conferences or seminars where women members are present. They tend to be isolated, deferred to, and treated with a ceremonial courtesy that does nothing to reduce what is quite often evident discomfort. At meals, which in any culture are especially significant times, they face either one of two reactions, depending on the rituals to which the other members of the conference are accustomed in their own companies. Either they are isolated – I have frequently observed a single woman delegate in a conference hotel eating alone while the rest of the dining room was full of

eagerly conversing male colleagues. Or they form the focus of
a group all eager to buy drinks, summon waiters, and being
excessively attentive. The similarity of this behaviour to courtship rituals makes misunderstanding possible, but it should be
noted that the reactions occur irrespective of the physical appearance of the woman concerned.

Isolation and over-attentiveness are both fear reactions. Isolation is the taboo at its simplest and strongest, over-attention
a more sophisticated attempt to placate the feared spirit by
ritually incorporating it into the group.

The taboo, most obvious on group occasions like these,
manifests itself at other times too. No manager feels happy at
meeting a stranger alone. Where the stranger is a man of
power, a consultant or perhaps an accountant, he will feel even
more uneasy. But where the stranger is a woman he is almost
certain to ensure that he is not alone, but has an assistant or
colleague present. Sometimes he will use a female assistant as
a counter-charm, but this is rare. Even females who are on the
same side are a potential danger. The thought of being out-
numbered by women at a meeting is more than most managers
can face.

So far I have been talking about the reaction to women who,
by entering management, have already broken a major taboo.
But most of the women the manager meets and deals with are
not colleagues or rivals, but women who have accepted the
status and roles that the culture assigns them. They are secretaries, typists, clerks, or they supervise women staff.

Contact with women in such roles is normal. Yet the contact
is still a dangerous one. So a complex and subtle structure of
rituals and taboos has been built up. Essential business can go
ahead, while the more dangerous forms of contact are avoided.
The system reaches its height with the development of the
most crucial relationship of all in business – that between the
boss and his secretary.

Very few institutions are as misunderstood and misinterpreted by outsiders as this relationship. The affair between the
secretary and her boss, and its ramification into the boss-wife-
secretary triangle, are a standby of contemporary business fiction. In the world of television and the novel, business men

take their secretaries on business trips, sleep with them, even on occasion marry them. In the real world it doesn't happen – or at least rarely, and then furtively and guiltily as befits people who are conscious of breaking their society's strongest taboo. With other people's secretaries, or with other secretaries' bosses, affairs are possible. As long as they aren't manifest in working hours, the only relevant rules are those observed by society in general. But the relationship between boss and secretary is so hedged about with taboos that it even applies outside the business environment.

It has to be so. For the relationship has to be an intimate one. They have to be alone together, know a great deal about each other's private lives, habits and tastes. Even in her simplest activities, like taking dictation, the secretary is an extension of her boss. Between them therefore all the normal taboos that safeguard individuals from contacting each other, especially men and women, have to be broken. In the management philosophy this obviously is a dangerous situation for both of them and, by the processes of contagion, for the rest of their community.

The relationship that ensues was christened by Ernest Crawley in *The Mystic Rose*. (Like *The Golden Bough*, it is too metaphysical for current anthropological taste, but still fascinating.) Crawley called it *ngia ngiampe*, the term used by the Australian Narrinyeri people to describe two people who, because they must come into close contact with each other, are made stringently taboo to each other. Everywhere among primitive peoples the basic elements are the same in the boss-secretary relationship. Two people who would normally be mutually taboo in what one might as well call an orthodox way, but who are forced by circumstance to break that taboo, can only do so by the substitution of yet more stringent prohibitions.

Thus unless he is consciously taking risks, a manager will avoid being alone with a woman on business affairs. It is taboo. Outside business hours he may take the same woman out, sleep with her, form a liaison, marry her. With his secretary, precisely the reverse is true. Inside the office they are necessarily intimate. (Strictly, physical contact between them is even more embarrassing than between two people who are not *ngia ngi-ampe*.) Outside the business environment they must not associate with each other.

Just occasionally the taboo is broken. But even where a single man marries his single secretary, and none of the normal conventions are broken, the effect on the manager as manager is considerable. He is marked out as an infected person, one whose managerial virility must be suspect, and that can be a damning suspicion. It is almost impossible to live down within the company. Normally the only way in which he can restore his position is by moving to another company where his indiscretion is unknown.

Since I first drafted this chapter, a friend has shown me an instance of a manager who is currently breaking this very taboo. It is the only such instance I have observed. Some of the circumstances are illuminating. In the first place both of them are single. They are not breaking any rules of conduct of the outside society. In fact, the relationship is known to the girl's parents, and to her outside friends (which is how I know about it). However, they have gone to great lengths to keep their meetings secret from their colleagues at the office. But the effect of this situation is significant. The manager is showing what would normally be diagnosed as signs of job dissatisfaction. He expresses discontent at the stagnation of his firm, complains about class barriers to promotion, and has applied for one or two other jobs. During his previous engagement to another girl who was not working in industry at all, he had manifested none of this behaviour.

It seems utterly impossible for a man to marry his secretary, and have her continue in the job. This would involve such a shattering of the taboo structure that it cannot even be imagined. To marry, or have an affair with, a former secretary, is more permissible, though it may raise eyebrows. If two people do find themselves unnaturally attracted – unnaturally from the managerial point of view: the situation resembles incest – it is conventional for the woman to leave her job. Once sufficient time has elapsed, and the longer they have worked together the longer it must be, they can perhaps pursue their liaison without recrimination or risk.

There are definite rituals of intimacy which mark the normal boss-secretary relationship: presenting flowers and gifts, preparing food and drinks, and so on. They can occasion jealousy among husbands and wives, but ironically they only serve to underline the severity of the taboo. Special sharing of this kind is everywhere the hall-mark of the *ngia ngiampe* relationship. Among the Narrinyeri the two people concerned exchange their preserved umbilical cords, their *kalduke*. Elsewhere the exchange may be less picturesque, but there is always some equivalent exchange.

How far the situation can be misunderstood even within the management culture was brought home to me many years ago. A friend of mine left his company, and took a more senior job. Automatically be began to treat his new secretary in the way that he would have done in his old company. But though the firms were in the same industry, and the two jobs in equivalent departments, their internal cultures were markedly different. In particular, the rituals of boss-secretary intimacy were very much more formal in the new company. Surnames for instance were invariably used, and presents restricted to birthdays and Christmas. Meals together were unheard of.

Naturally enough, my friend broke all the rules. His secretary, equally new to the company, responded appropriately. As it happened, I had a business connection with the department, and therefore had known most of his subordinates longer than he had himself. Within only a few weeks three of them had, independently, taken me aside and told me how worried they were about the 'affair' my friend was having with his secretary, and the effect it might have on his career. Not his marriage, incidentally. I told them I knew they were mistaken (I did know), but it did nothing to reassure them. They thought I was covering up.

What is interesting is that he was a great success in his job. If he was having an affair, it didn't affect his decision-making. But they were certain it would, and they went on being certain until he left the company a couple of years later with none of their forebodings having come to pass.

Nowhere else in management do sexual taboos reach this extreme of subtlety or stringency, although there are sometimes elements of the *ngia ngiampe* relationship between managers and other close female subordinates. Generally the sexes are segregated as much as possible. Access to typing pools is normally restricted. The sexes tend to eat separately in staff canteens. Even the institution of the typing pool, and especially the use of dictating machines and the emergence of the 'audio-typist' who never even sees the man whose voice she hears, are phenomena that frequently seem to be due more to an attempt to lessen intersexual contact than to any efforts to economise or improve efficiency.

Usually too it goes against convention to bring womenfolk, including wives and mistresses, into the office, except on ritually approved occasions. Much the same defensive behaviour occurs at conferences and seminars; and if it happens too often the manager concerned is likely to gain a reputation for effeminacy. Sometimes the wife, or the close female kin, of a popular or successful manager will find that far from being avoided, she will be offered drinks or food. Fairly obviously this is an attempt at a rite of incorporation, with the object of binding the donor indirectly to the manager himself and sharing his good fortune. It is likely that a similar motive would underlie any attempt to seduce the manager's wife. The attraction of contagious good fortune outweighs the more rational risk of retribution.

While the fear of contagious effeminacy is always present, it would be wrong to assume that a reputation for sexual prowess is harmful to a manager. On the contrary, with certain stipulations, it can enhance his image. In any predominantly masculine culture where emotions are more influential than reason the Casanova figure is a respected one, and a reputation for success with women is an important element in building up the charisma that a popular leader must have. It is important however that the manager be demonstrably successful in his job, so that it is obvious that his virility has been maintained. For this to happen in spite of frequent association with women he must, in the popular view, command abnormal power.

He must also be a lay manager, not an accountant. Gifted with more power than ordinary men, the accountant is also more vulnerable. Closer to the supernatural forces, he is also more likely to attract their attention. Thus it is even more incumbent on him to avoid egregious behaviour. His special skills are also particularly masculine. He is therefore more vulnerable than others to the threat of feminine contagion. None of this is particularly abnormal for a priestly caste.

Finally, the use of managerial time or other resources in pursuit of sexual ends is a violation of the primary code of the culture. Not only is it a blatant assertion of idleness, it is a denial that the purpose of the manager is to make a profit for the company. As such it is a straightforward invitation to re-tribution – sparked perhaps by the jealousy of the gods.

11. Saturnalia

Sometime towards the end of 1966 an edict went out from the central management of a large British corporation to the effect that Christmas parties at which alcohol was consumed should no longer be held on company premises. Partly a response to government propaganda against drunken driving, the ban was due to the temporary ascendancy at corporate headquarters of a puritanical sect among the directorate. The formal association of the company with festivity of any kind was anathema.

Reception of the edict was varied, but the major effect was to provide the heads of subsidiary companies with a new weapon in their ongoing campaign against the central bureacracy. At no loss to themselves they could enforce the ban, make plain their own opposition to it, and thereby increase the popular antipathy to the centre. Some among them gained even more popularity by risking open defiance of the ban themselves, or by turning a blind eye on the transgressions of their subordinates.

The results of the ban were minimal. Even in the more disciplined parts of the company, as in the headquarters offices themselves, the most that was achieved was the removal of the celebrations to a nearby pub or hired room. Work disruption reached about the same level as usual.

Apart from showing how far the appearance of authority may be divorced from reality, the story raises two questions. Why should the habit of holding office parties at Christmas have arisen in the first place? And why should it have become so deeply ingrained and popular that managers should risk ignoring or violating the edict?

Some insights can be gained from observing other cultures in which taboo systems play a prominent part, particularly where the dominant official religion is at odds with the actual magico-religious beliefs and practices of the people.

Regular festivities at which the normal rules of behaviour are relaxed are commonplace throughout the world. The Roman Saturnalia are the best-known example, but the same release is apparent in accounts of the medieval Feast of Fools, the election of mock kings in Upper Egypt, May Day and Carnival celebrations in Europe, South America and the Caribbean, and festivals of various kinds among the Australians, Malays and the peoples of the Pacific. Even in the Chinese and Hindu cultures the institution existed and to some extent still exists. As in an 1876 account of India: 'The festival of Holi marks the arrival of spring, and is held in honour of the goddess Holica, or Vasanti, who personifies that season in the Hindu Pantheon. The carnival lasts several days during which time the most licentious debauchery and disorder reign throughout every class of society. It is the regular Saturnalia of India. Persons of the greatest respectability, without regard to rank or age, are not ashamed to take part in the orgies which mark this season of the year.'

In some societies such periods of freedom from restraint occur whenever disaster is imminent. However, as a rule they are annual. It is therefore impossible to explain them satisfactorily without some reference to the yearly rotation of the seasons. Indeed there is a simple theory about such festivals, especially in so far as they encourage promiscuity. According to this they are mainly rites of sympathetic magic to secure the fertility of the land. However, this explanation does not account for all the features of such festivities. Nor does it explain their persistence in cultures which no longer accept that particular magical belief or are not dependent on agricultural fertility.

Another theory treats such occasions as rites of passage, symbolizing the transition from one year to another (or from one month or day to another). Between the old and the new there is a period of transition in which the normal rules of conduct no longer apply. But this theory also doesn't provide an explanation of the reason *why* such festivals should appear to meet a virtually universal need. This need has been explained in two ways. Since the explanations do not conflict, they may well both be true.

If taboos are to maintain their protective effect, they must be periodically and ritually broken. Sir James Frazer invented the analogy which compares taboo to electrical charge – the person who is taboo has accumulated supernatural energy against which others must be insulated. Carrying the analogy further, if the charge builds up too greatly there may be a catastrophic breakdown. It must therefore be periodically discharged when circumstances are safe. Such circumstances are provided, for instance, by the transitional period between one year and the next, a phase outside normal time when ordinary dangers no longer threaten – in Indo-China even the spirits of the dead join the festivities.

The other explanation stresses the recurring need for an expression of the solidarity of the community. To meet that need, the contact that is normally prevented by the taboo structure is ritually enforced by eating and drinking together, by handshake, embrace, kiss, intercourse, and playing team games. (Most of the more popular sports have their origin in games that were played on such occasions.) This explanation also accounts for similar celebrations likely to take place when the community is faced by some calamity; for at such times the individual's need for support by the group is strongest.

With the last two explanations we come close to understanding why the management culture is permeated with the institution of the office party and equivalent rituals. Indeed the official reason for office parties is to 'bring people together', 'make them feel like one big family', 'foster a sense of identity', and so on. As such they are, of course, frequently sneered at, and I suspect with good reason. For the managers miss the full point. The Saturnalia does build a sense of union, but a Saturnalia where people are on their best behaviour is a contradiction in terms. It can't work. Yet that is precisely what many parties attempt to be, and why they fail to achieve their object.

Office parties, works outings, annual dinners, and so on will only be of use if the normal taboos are not only ignored but broken. Physical contact, especially between the sexes, sharing of food and drink between people who normally are barred from mingling, free expression of criticism and hostility, common access to normally taboo places – these are necessary events if the tensions built up by the continuous observation of taboos are not to reach unbearable heights.

Some companies recognize it. More frequently it is understood in some parts of a company, and they may gain a reputation for periodic licentiousness. (I know one company where this reputation is pre-eminently held by the accountants' department. I don't think this damages my characterization of accountants as priests – the greater the everyday taboos that have to be observed, the greater the need for recurrent release.)

All too often, however, the need for 'togetherness' is realized but superficially. The underlying truth is ignored. Gatherings take place at which the usual taboos, instead of being broken, are reinforced. Ritual respect is given to seniors, intersexual relationships are meticulously polite, physical contact is avoided.

This kind of behaviour is common in firms with a long tradition of family ownership, especially where the family maintains a reputation for paternalism. When, to everyone's surprise, human relations do erupt in such a firm they tend to do so much more violently than in companies with a tradition of labour troubles. Part of the reason may well lie in the absence of occasions when the taboos are broken.

I have noticed another occasional tendency in small family firms where the family is conscious of its status. Taboo-breaking gatherings are held without the family. In one such company I used to know (it is now defunct) the 'office' parties included wives, girl friends, boy friends, business contacts, rivals, and even on occasion total strangers. They are still nostalgically remembered. But the company had also one of the widest gaps between the owner and his staff that I have ever observed.

Though by some criteria the company was largely successful, ultimately it lost money. No one was trying to make any, except the owner. The organization was co-operative, loyal, and highly motivated. Indeed, it was one of the most cohesive I have come across. But only to achieving its own ends.

For many managers, especially senior ones, the taboos of personal isolation, of proper respect, of inconspicuous and noncontentious behaviour, together with the dogma of maximum profit, are so deeply ingrained that they cannot face the need to break them. For such people it is probably better not to have office gatherings at all. To that extent the company I quoted at the beginning of the chapter might have been right, except that a tradition of effective unifying parties had existed in some units which had recently been taken over, and at lower organization levels generally. As a result a large number of people felt deeply, not that a *privilege* had been taken away, but that they were denied an essential element of their necessary expressive rituals. Their reaction was deeply emotional. And it was out of that strong resentment that the subsidiary chief executives made much political capital.

Occasionally, one comes across a department, even a whole company, where such tension-releasing rituals are not necessary, because the unit is free of taboos. I once attempted to create such a department myself, with mixed success. It isn't easy, nor perhaps is it often advisable, for several reasons. To start with, the normal managerial taboos have their point, even if it is sometimes blunted. Where an operation is fairly routine and predictable, taboos help to increase efficiency. Through their influence people are conditioned to act correctly and quickly. Their choice of action is fast and untroubled by irrelevant doubts, or even the need to think. Everyone knows their place.

But taboos tend to get in the way of a unit that is exploring new areas of any kind, or faced by a rapidly changing environment. In such cases eliminating them may be desirable; but it is difficult.

In fact, if the people concerned are already used to operating together, it verges on the impossible. Some behavioural scientists, particularly those who have developed T-groups and the kinds of contact therapy pioneered at the Esalon institute, try to eliminate such taboos. I have known a fair number of managers who as individuals have benefited from such treatment. Nevertheless, the treatment has rarely produced any strong or long-term alteration in the behaviour of a group. Instead it tends to function as taboo-discharge ritual, on the model of the Saturnalia. As such it is useful, but when the normal environment once again surrounds the individuals –

when they are back in 'real' time – the normal behaviour patterns gradually reassert themselves.

The only real chance is with a group the members of which are new to one another, and come from relatively taboo-free environments or environments in which they themselves have been misfits. It is possible, but highly uncommon, for someone to live in a complex taboo structure and remain unaffected by it. And to take someone who is used to the comforting stability of such a structure, and place him in a situation where he has neither this nor any reasonable alternative, can be a distressing experience.

Let us assume a group has been created which is highly flexible in its behaviour. Yet the contact with the rest of the organization is likely to be a source of continuous abrasion. By definition, the group is behaving in a conspicuously different manner. It is attracting attention, which is enough to worry orthodox members of the culture. The group is also very likely to be unconcerned about appearing idle from time to time, and to be as openly critical in dealing with people outside as they are among themselves. Both of these are breaches of primary taboos which will upset even those who may recognize the value of the work the group is producing.

Such a situation cannot last. Either such groups are 're-organized' out of existence, or they are encysted by taboos that isolate them as a group from the rest of the organization, and prevent their producing any really useful work.

There may be an answer, but I have not yet come across it. It may be possible to create such a group in an organization so that its effect on the rest is minimized. At the moment I suspect that the only way a taboo-free culture can exist is as a totally independent entity, and a fairly small one.

And as long as companies are dominated by taboos it is best to allow for the importance of Saturnalia.

START
HERE

12. Sacrae Personae

Most managers are taboo to the rest of their community at some time or other. A few are in a permanent state of taboo – those who are in such close contact with supernatural forces that it is always dangerous to be near them. The taboo structure protects others from their power. It also helps to maintain the exalted in a pure and undefiled state. Otherwise they themselves will not be able to control the powers that they personify, and themselves be in serious danger.

This separation of the leader from his followers is frequently misinterpreted. For Shakespeare's Claudius 'such divinity doth hedge a king' in order to make him safe from treasonable attack. But the forces feared are supernatural. Any survey of the multitudinous practices that have evolved in almost every society make it obvious. At one time in Ethiopia the Emperor had four officers who had to clothe themselves exactly like him. 'When the King of Boni sits, all sit; when he rises all rise; should he ride and fall from his horse, all must fall from their horses likewise; when he bathes, all his courtiers must bathe too ... In Uganda, if the king laughs, all the courtiers laugh, if he sneezes, all sneeze ...'

These instances are taken from *The Mystic Rose*. The attempt of the ritual was to mislead supernatural forces by making it impossible to tell who was the real king. Such devices, no matter how primitive the society, could hardly be a practical method of protecting the king from physical attack. Assassins are not as easily confused as spirits.

It also seems unlikely that physical protection was the reason for the proscriptions that Lucy Mair describes surrounding the king of the Nyoro. He 'had to be present every morning at the milking of the nine cattle specially dedicated to him, and then to drink some of the new milk ... people concerned in the cooking and serving of his food also had to be in a state of ritual purity. The girls who churned the royal milk had to be virgins, the boy who herded his nine cattle had to be below the age of puberty, the men who cooked his food had to abstain from sexual intercourse. Like many other African kings he ate alone.'

So did the Pope for that matter, according to Frederick Elworthy's 1895 collection of superstitions, *The Evil Eye*, which also contains many instances of kings who were not allowed to be seen except by a specially elect few of their people.

Sometimes such taboos are strictly restricted to the person of the king himself. Sometimes they relate to his whole family, sometimes to an entire noble caste, in varying degrees of intensity. Among the Polynesians, *mana* is a mystical power which every man possesses in some measure – the more important and politically powerful the man, the greater his *mana* and the greater the taboos against contact.

In management the details of the taboos surrounding the chief executive vary greatly in detail. They may or may not be shared by his family, or the rest of the directorate. But one major principle seems to apply everywhere. The strength of the taboos increases with the proportion of shares owned by him. It is supreme when he is the major shareholder or owns the company outright. Bearing in mind that shareholding is more or less equivalent to divinity (see Chapter 2) this is hardly surprising.

I suspect that on both sides of the Atlantic the newspaper and magazine publishing industry is notorious for the strength of the taboos that surround its chief executives because of the fact that so much of the industry is owned by individuals or single families. No other distinguishing feature of the industry would account for it. Most people in the industry have become so used to the deference that is or has been paid to the great Press figures – from Northcliffe, Beaverbrook, Hearst and Luce down to Thomson, the Berrys, the Astors and the Chandlers – that exactly the same pattern of taboo surrounded Cecil King at least in the last few years of his chairmanship of I P C, even though he was only a minimal shareholder.

Therefore, as is traditional in the industry, he lived in ritual seclusion, with his own kitchen and dining room in his office suite. Even the members of the directorate worried in case he should be kept waiting. They were concerned to ensure that nothing controversial should be said in his presence. In particular there was a strong taboo that nothing pessimistic about the future should be said. Such remarks were in the jargon of the company, considered 'defeatist'. The few people who had access to him at all regularly would rehearse with each other what they were going to say when they talked to him. The rehearsal would become even more intense when a member of the directorate was to be accompanied by an uninitiated member of his own staff.

I quote this as an example of common behaviour strongly reminiscent of the barriers that exist between primitive kings and their subjects. The only slight exception is the one already referred to, namely that Cecil King was treated with the degree of attention normally reserved for chief executives who are also major shareholders. But then he was, of course, the nephew of one of the great demigods of the industry. Although the sister's son relationship is not particularly recognized in English law, in many primitive societies it is the most important blood tie of all.

It would be unfair to assume that this behaviour was desired by King, or even noticed. It was an automatic response of the community which he led.

A full recital of the variety of detailed taboos operating around the chief executives of industry would be too long. However, certain characteristics seem to crop up almost everywhere.

Dissension is well-hidden from the chief executive. It is, as I have already described, taboo at any management meeting, but greater precautions are taken to ensure that nobody says anything controversial in front of the chief. On occasion one courtier may attempt privately to subvert another by whispering in the chief's ear. But criticisms will never be launched publicly. And even privately they are likely to take the form 'You know I've always liked X . . .'

Eating is an occasion of special ritual in all cultures. Everywhere there are groups – castes, orders, ranks, clans – whose

members may not eat with outsiders, and individuals who must
eat alone. Among some South American and African tribes
every person must eat alone and unobserved; in part of Mada-
gascar, behind locked doors. Since the management culture
sets such store by the power of the communal meal as a rite of
incorporation, the taboo cannot go to such extreme lengths.
However, where a chief executive is also the owner he normally eats alone. Where there are two or three major shareholders active in the company, they will eat together. In both
cases they will also have fairly frequent ritual meals with
members of the directorate, and, less often, attend ritual meals
with lower levels of management.

In public companies whose chief executive is not a major
shareholder frequent eating and drinking together of the directorate is one way of ritually emphasizing that the chief executive is only *primus inter pares*. His sacredness tends to be
shared. Such conviviality also formally emphasizes the distinction between the directorate and the rest of the company. In
owner-managed companies the distinction between directorate
and general management is likely to be blurred; they may well
eat together.

Excretory processes are, to the savage at least, closely linked
with eating, and subject to the same taboos. It is interesting
that this closely parallels the practice in management. Groups
that eat together will also have common lavatory facilities, and
individuals who normally eat alone in their offices are also
supplied with their own toilet facilities.

Driving is normally taboo for the chief executive (and the
directorate) at least on official journeys, but frequently on all
occasions. A chauffeur is an essential member of his personal
staff who will also have the task of preventing him from defiling himself by carrying objects apart from perhaps the ritual
briefcase. (Only when the role of the chauffeur is seen in its
true light does the ceremonial habit of lending one's chauffeur
to an honoured guest reveal its full meaning. The host indicates that he has lesser need for ritual protection as the guest
commands more powerful forces, and thus is surrounded by
stronger taboos. Declining the offer returns the compliment.)

Wasting time is similarly taboo to the chief executive. Here the general taboo against over-idleness is taken to extremes. Elaborate precautions will be taken always to make sure that the chief executive never wastes a moment on anything except the important company rituals. He must not have to wait for a plane or a train. He must not be kept waiting by outsiders. If his car breaks down another must be rushed to the spot. His subordinates must be precisely on time for meetings.

To anyone outside the culture, the amount of effort, time and money spent to ensure that this particular taboo is observed is literally incredible. It is one reason why the minimum staff of the chief executive of an average-sized company is two secretaries, a personal assistant and a chauffeur.

There is another taboo that accounts for the size of his personal staff. Of course the chief executive must from time to time meet people, but never unpreparedly and, ideally, never alone. They must be ritually attuned for the meeting through a series of formal verbal exchanges with the staff, a carefully calculated amount of time spent in one or more waiting rooms. (It will depend on the status of the visitor.) In essence this preparation ritual is a rite of passage. It has a standard form. This includes a rite of separation from the outside world, which usually takes place between the visitor and the secretary; a transitional period of purification spent in isolation; and a rite of incorporation, when he is finally brought to see the chief executive. This last rite may be as perfunctory as a handshake, or include drinking together and even eating. What matters is that the visitor has been sufficiently purified by the ritual to ensure that neither the chief executive nor he himself suffers from the contact.

It may have become apparent already that the so-called 'status symbols' are in fact nothing of the kind. It is missing a vital truth to believe that the trappings surrounding the chief executive, or any manager, are solely to proclaim his status. Nor do they exist primarily to boost his self-esteem, though they may well do that incidentally. I would agree that they have no pragmatic business value. They may indeed even be a handicap to efficient or effective working. But they do have a purpose. Within the confines of management philosophy it is an important one. They serve to maintain a ritual distance between the chief executive and those with whom contact would be both dangerous and defiling.

Now the importance of the size of the executive's desk appears in its true light, as increasing the physical barrier necessary to observe the taboo, and protect both parties. That the really powerful executive may have no desk at all does not disprove this hypothesis. It only happens where the rites of passage are complex and efficacious enough to ensure that the visitor is purified before he enters the room.

As one ascends the hierarchy such ritual barriers increase in strength. The initiation rites that occur at each of the transitions are themselves indications that a major change in the powers of the individual is taking place. The feared power, the *mana*, of the executive is a function of his office rather than of the man himself.

However, within each grade each individual must demonstrate the relative strength of his *mana*. The amount of ceremony with which he will be surrounded, depends on his success which also decides the likelihood of his selection for incorporation into a higher grade.

Among some people, such power is demonstrated by the effectiveness of their instrumental magic. Thus according to Lucy Mair in *Primitive Government*, among the Alur, 'the power of chiefs is called *ker,* but this is not conceived as a power that can be given or taken through any performance of ritual. It is simply known by its fruits. If a chief prospers, and rain falls when he prays for it, this shows that he has *ker*; if he does not have *ker* he ought not to be a chief, and in the old days this would be a reason for neighbouring peoples who had recently accepted an Alur chief to go to his father and request another of his sons in his place.' (It is worth noting that *ker* is an inherited quality. It is restricted to the chiefly lineages, even if all members of those lineages may not possess it.)

Many peoples want to see this kind of assessment of a person's *mana* (to revert to the more familiar Polynesian term) applied in management. They call it 'results-oriented performance appraisal'. Indeed, there are lots of managers who will ritually intone, and believe, 'In this company we go by results'. As an article of explicit faith it is more common in the U S than in Britain, where apparently other factors than demonstrable success count in achieving promotion. British managers will admit to believing that results count more in American companies. I suspect the distinction is not as great as is popularly supposed. Conformity to ritual is a more important factor in the majority of companies in both countries.

In any case the difference is irrelevant to my major point: judgement by results is not as empirical as it seems. Consider more closely what happens among the Alur. The chief performs the necessary rain-making rituals. Either it rains or it doesn't. If it does the chief is considered to have *ker*; if it doesn't, he hasn't. From our superior vantage point we can see that the conclusion is unjustified. What is being rewarded is not supernatural power, but coincidence. What is being punished is not lack of power, but bad luck.

If this were true in management too, it might not be so bad. Better a lucky leader than an unlucky one. In the same way there is some merit in the belief that an important quality in a cricket captain is his ability to win the toss. But the trouble is that in management even the results are not clearly beneficial or clearly bad. Whatever the outcome of a particular enterprise, it is always possible to argue that it could have been worse, or it could have been better. It is never possible to establish beyond doubt what would have happened if a manager had acted in a different manner.

Moreover, the actual recording of success is frequently, if not always, a matter of opinion. The Penn-Central failure, the Leasco-Pergamon affair, the I O S collapse, the G E C-A E I merger are only some of the most blatant examples of the truth that one man's 'profit' is another man's 'loss'. Even in the apparently simple matter of assessing the performance of, say, a mutual fund, the subjective variables blur the picture irremediably. For instance, in 1969 it was possible for I O S to claim that its International Investment Trust had grown at 14 per cent per annum, but equally possible to argue that the true figure was 5·9 per cent, depending on whether the base year was taken as 1960 when the Trust was first launched, or 1962 when it was reorganized. Over the long term, there is no reason to suppose that investment trusts in either the U S or

Britain have done on average any better or worse than the
market index. As *Fortune* once pointed out, the fund managers might just as well have gone fishing as busied themselves
with buying and selling. Yet reputations have been both made
and broken on the operation of what objectively seems to have
been simple chance.

Inside a company the problem is even worse, since managers
operate within a framework of 'company policy' which limits
their freedom of decision. It is possible to argue reasonably
convincingly that any poor performance was due to the ham-
pering effects of policy restrictions. A common example arises
where one division buys from another at a transfer price laid
down by the central headquarters. The buying division can
always claim that it could have bought cheaper elsewhere, and
the selling division that it could get higher prices outside the
company. (Sometimes, such a transfer price is biased markedly
in favour of one division, and then only one division has an
excuse. More usually, however, every attempt is made to ensure that the price is fair. Then both sides can complain.) In
theory of course such a transfer can be made at 'market value',
but the theory is only applicable in the free markets of classical
economics. And they are rather difficult to find.

The objective appraisal used by the Alur, chancy though it
may be, is not possible in management. Therefore other
methods need to be found of establishing whether or not an
executive has the requisite *mana*. The most common method is
observation of how strictly he observes the general taboos of
behaviour described in Chapters 9 and 10.

Thus the manager with *mana* is decisive. If the correctness
of a man's decisions is rarely estimable, the speed with which he
makes them is. Speed is therefore substituted as a criterion of
merit. Similarly the manager with *mana* is terse. His memo-
randa are brief and to the point. He is impatient both of cir-
cumlocutions and of lengthy analyses and justifications.

It is interesting to note that after his victory in the 1970
General Election, every effort was made to demonstrate that
Edward Heath possessed this executive *mana*. Up till then he
had generally been considered to have the least innate power
of any recent British political leader. His victory apparently

showed that this impression must be wrong. Thus it became necessary to ascribe to him all the attributes of the possessor of great executive power. Supporters, opponents and neutrals felt driven to do so, in order to maintain their essential world-view. Thus Anthony Sampson could write in the overtly neutral but if anything anti-Conservative *Observer*: 'Then after a minute or so he comes out with a decision, and that's it ... he sends out brisk minutes with a Churchillian brevity, though without the eloquence ... His speeches, like his minutes, are uncompromising and bare ... he shuts his mouth firmly, his lips doggedly together.' In the same passage, Heath is contrasted with his defeated rival, whose own lack of *mana* must now be established: 'Wilson loves talking; Heath prefers silence. Wilson naturally avoids decisions; Heath *likes* taking them. Wilson encouraged a certain vagueness; Heath likes precision.'

If the election had gone differently, as everyone expected, it would have had to be the other way round. For this is far from being simply a matter of the projection of a desirable political image. It is a question of preserving the integrity of the society's creed of executive success.

Politics and management do not always share the same magico-religious beliefs. In Britain and Europe they are moving closer together. In America they are moving apart. But on one point there is agreement between the continents. Managerial ability is assessed by observing how closely a person conforms to the stereotype of the successful manager. Managers who conform are promoted. And since promotion is equated with success, a logically circular process ensues which makes the rule self-justifying – a useful attribute of any magical principle.

As I pointed out in the Introduction, it is noticeable how such behaviour patterns are automatically adopted by participants in role-playing exercises on management courses, and how non-standard behaviour can seriously upset observers even though in such abstract situations there can be no rational fear of contagion or retribution. This could not be so if the taboos that surround senior managers, and the qualities that are associated with executive *mana*, were not believed to be magically necessary. It would be different if senior managers were not believed to be touched with supernatural power, to be, in the conventional language I used for the title of this chapter, *sacrae personae*.

Unfortunately for the logic that makes success depend upon *mana*, and the possession and preservation of *mana* depend upon the observation of a specific ritual pattern of behaviour, these assumptions just are not true. Some of the most successful individuals in business have notably and habitually violated managerial taboos. And from an unbiased viewpoint, meticulous observance of taboo frequently produces mediocrity if not failure.

Somehow, the successful breakers of taboo have to be accounted for. A place has to be found for them in the management cosmology. What that place is, and how it fits in with orthodox management beliefs, is the subject of the next chapter.

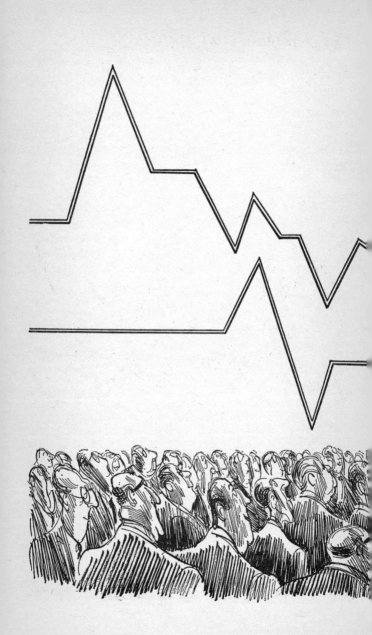

13. Demigods and Heroes

As I have already pointed out, management is no exception to the rule that while all magical rituals find their justification in logic, they derive their authority from myth. Literary-minded critics have tended to see myths as representing garbled history or garbled science. Malinowski was perhaps the first modern anthropologist to emphasize that myths provided 'charters' for present action. The difference in interpretation shows a switch in major concern. Malinowski was not interested in the content or style of mythological accounts but mainly in the effect they had on the culture, and the reasons for which they were told.

For him a myth is the story of the first doing of some act that is still repeated in ritual, or of the origin of some facet of social structure or behaviour. It provides 'the effective precedent of a glorified past for repetitive actions in the present'.

Thus the veneration paid to monkeys in India is based on the Hindu myth of the assistance given by Hanuman, the monkey-god, to Rama, one of the incarnations of Vishnu, and the caste-system is accounted for by the creation of the different castes from different parts of the body of Brahma. The Inca custom of boring and enlarging the ear-lobes follows the myth that Ayar Cachi, when he instructed his brothers, the first Incas, to build a city at Cuzco, told them always to bore their ears as a mark that they should be honoured and feared by their people. Among the Greeks, the fact that the mysteries of the Earth-Mother were celebrated at Eleusis was accounted for by the tale that there she wept in her long search for her daughter Persephone, and there too she first taught the use of the plough, the sickle and the spade to Triptolemus.

Myths are answers to the most demanding question of all, 'Why did it all start?' All bodies of mythology contain myths of origin (if not always myths of deliberate creation). Occasionally managers, too, question their origin, and a myth exists to account for the fact that we have organizations, in particular business organizations. The myth is unusual, though not unique, in that it has not crystallized into a tale about a single hero, but various forms with different heroes. It can however be told anonymously in its radical form. Told in such manner I like to call it the 'gaffer' myth, though I admit to stealing the epithet from Stafford Beer, who uses it in telling the tale as part of the complex creed of cybernetics. It goes like this:

Once upon a time there was a man who owned a business. He made things and sold them. Thus he made a living. But as time went by, he found he could sell more things than he made, so he employed assistants to help him produce more. Then he found that he was spending all his time selling, and none making. So he employed a salesman, then a book-keeper, and so on. He had become a 'gaffer' – a boss, an employer. Business continued to expand. Instead of a handful of employees, he soon had dozens. Instead of one salesman, one book-keeper, and a few production hands all directly supervised by himself, he had several salesmen, several book-keepers, several groups of production workers. To take charge of each group he was forced to invent the manager. In the fullness of time, as the business grew still further, he invented the hierarchical organisation. Which, children, is why your daddy is a salesman who works for a sales manager who works for a divisional sales director who works for a group marketing director who works for a managing director who works for The Chairman.

Like all the best myths, it is convincing. One has to admit there may be an element of truth in it. But from the point of view of realistic history it is rather unlikely that it ever happened just like that. It is certainly an atypical story. Even if one restricts oneself to the narrow field of manufacturing industry, and furthermore to the period of the Industrial Revolution in Britain, to gain the most favourable conditions for finding such stories, they are rare to say the least. I have never managed to find any, though I am willing to concede they may exist. The vast majority of enterprises appear to have been founded as partnerships, and had employer–employee relationships from the very start.

If they grew, they grew just as companies do nowadays, by

take-overs, mergers, licensing agreements with other firms and an array of other methods, none of which correspond with the universal creation myth. Even Clarke & Rockefeller, Produce & Commission, 32 River St, Cleveland, started out as a partnership with staff, and they were only selling farm and household goods. The manipulations that turned it into Standard Oil of Ohio involved finding other partners and undercutting competitors and taking them over. John D. Rockefeller was never a 'gaffer' in that sense.

It wouldn't matter very much, except as a matter of academic curiosity, were it not for the fact that the 'gaffer' myth is used to explain and justify the centralized hierarchical control system, and, by the cyberneticists especially, to categorize the company as an organic entity which is really only the extension of a single individual's nervous system. It therefore becomes important to point out that the myth has no historical basis. Organizations of people have always existed. The primary need for them is not rooted in the fact that there is more work than one man can do. It stems from the differences between individuals – differences in skills, abilities and intellectual power, but also differences in preferences, attitudes, and even moral standards.

Still, the myth exists, and it is used to explain and justify. It is also relevant to point out that the tales managers tell of heroes almost always contain traces of the 'gaffer' myth. And for this there is good reason.

Almost every magico-religious culture has supernatural beings and tales of mortals who achieved divine or semi-divine status. The supernatural beings of the management culture include the class of shareholders, as I explained in Chapter 2. The demigods are majority shareholders or outright owners of successful companies. Their supernatural powers are measured by the size of the fortune they acquire.

In some cases the power is so small that it is demonstrably less than that of a senior manager in a rich company. It may seem odd to Western ears to talk of weak demigods, or supernatural forces that can be overcome by mortals, as we are accustomed to a culture in which God is omnipotent, and all the other commonly recognized supernatural beings are more powerful than men. But this is a biased view. Cultures in which some spirits are seen as weaker than some men are common. The Guyanese *peaiman* whom I have already mentioned has the power to frighten away spirits, not by invoking a higher power, as the Catholic priest does in exorcism, but simply by using his own powers. *They* are frightened of *him*.

There are grounds therefore for allowing supernatural status and special powers to all owner-managers, even though any particular individual at any moment may be rather insignificant. And the management culture treats the 'entrepreneur' with an awe reserved for the semi-divine.

One natural result is the rise of local myths to account for the veneration of demigods who may be unheard of in the rest of the culture. Frequently such myths are told of the founder of the firm. They may even outlast the take-over of the firm by a more powerful company. From time to time this can lead to severe religious tension within the larger community, and even to active hostility should the rites celebrating the founder be forbidden. To change the name of a company which commemorates the founder will probably provoke a great deal of emotional upset and a consequent falling away in productivity.

Just so did the city-states of classical Greece tell myths of their foundation (frequently explaining the name of the city), and their reaction to occasional religious suppression was on a similar pattern. On the whole, however, their political leaders were too superstitious or too sensible to interfere with such things. They were more likely to incorporate the local myths into their own beliefs.

The great demigods of the management culture who are honoured everywhere, the equivalents of Theseus, Hercules, Perseus and Jason, are such men as Andrew Carnegie, John D. Rockefeller, Henry Ford, Lord Northcliffe, Lord Nuffield, Alfred Nobel – men who created and controlled vast empires and made immense fortunes in the process. The tales told of them almost always incorporate the 'gaffer' myth.

Thus the popular image of Ford and Nuffield is of an engineer working on his own account in a garden shed (Ford) or a disused school (Nuffield), making cars and gradually selling more and more of them, thus inevitably creating a large organization. The popular stories however overlook the fact that although Ford and Nuffield started that way, both their first attempts failed.

In 1903 Ford's third, and finally successful, effort was a joint enterprise with twelve stockholders and 28,000 dollars in cash. Nuffield's second try, in 1919, only came after he had closely studied Ford's methods. Within a year of starting he was up to dozens of cars a week.

As I said, the historical facts about the managerial demigods rarely match up to the myths. Furthermore such people must by definition have broken some of the standard managerial taboos. Frequently, indeed, they have hardly conformed to the stereotype of executive *mana* at all. Thus Sargent, after painting a portrait of Rockefeller, compared him to 'a sort of medieval saint, a Francis of Assisi'. And Alfred Nobel, inventor of dynamite and the Peace Prize, could be described as 'insignificant-looking ... small in stature, inconspicuous, self-effacing, colourless ... a cynical idealist, a brilliant conversationalist who preferred his own company, a lover of poetry who made pathetic attempts to write'. Neither description conforms at all closely to the prescribed standards of the successful manager.

It is interesting to see how the culture copes with this conflict. One thing it can do of course is to ignore the inconvenient facts. So, in telling the Edison myth at orthodox conferences, the speaker may emphasize that when Edison was at his productive peak he averaged only four hours' sleep a night. In the First World War, when informed that it would take nine months to build a carbolic acid plant he had designed he called his own chemical workers together, and worked with them to build it in seventeen days – and produce seven hundred pounds of acid on the next day. But the speaker is likely to leave out that one of Edison's earliest recorded inventions was a device that automatically sent out the hourly call sign he was supposed, as a telegraph operator, to make throughout the night, so that he could get some sleep. And to omit the interesting fact that the first use he made of his electric light bulbs was to light up his Menlo Park laboratories for a New Year's party for his friends.

The more subtle technique, however, is not to hide the broken taboos, but to emphasize them – to make it evident that such lapses are only permitted to men who have the touch of genius. Such genius makes them 'entrepreneurs'. It is O K to behave egregiously as long as you own the firm, or subsequently make enough money to buy it. It was permissible for Lord Nuffield during the 1921 slump to slash his prices. But the mortal manager is left in no doubt as to what would happen to him, if he did the same, rather than following orthodox procedures – laying off men, cutting back overheads, and waiting for the wrath of the gods to go away.

The manager is faced with a simple choice. He can break taboos, offend against the standards of the culture, and risk disaster in the attempt to achieve divinity – gambling that he has the required inexplicable supernatural power. Or he must observe the formalities and the rituals, sacrificing dreams of entrepreneurship for the sake of security and community, and a share in the power and status of the organization.

It is hardly surprising that there should be perennial complaints about the absence of entrepreneurship in management. According to the standards of the culture the entrepreneur is insane and is automatically rejected. Only if after rejection he succeeds in establishing a fortune will his insanity be recognized as a mark of divine favour.

Yet enough people appear to be prepared to brave the scorn of the established culture to provide a steady stream of new heroes. For it is one of the peculiarities of the management pantheon that a position in it can be achieved within one's own lifetime.

It was so with most of the examples I have already mentioned. It is true now of elder figures like Sir John Ellerman, Onassis and Howard Hughes. It is equally true of younger men like Jim Slater (an example of the unusual accountant-entrepreneur, the priest-hero), Hugh Heffner, and Saul Steinberg, around all of whom the clouds of myth are beginning to gather. Slater is even beginning to be cast, like the centaur Chiron, as a tutor of heroes. To have worked for Slater-Walker seems almost to have been established, at least by the British business press, as an automatic mark of divine favour, and an immediate qualification for success as a financial entrepreneur. Malcolm Horsman, of Ralli International, Herbert Despard, of Cannon Street Investments, Ron Shuck of Cornwall Properties, John Bentley of Barclay Securities, Richard Eldridge of Junitex – they were all at first seized upon by the Press as new heroes. They are notable taboo breakers. Eldridge, who has listed his hobbies, egregiously enough, as power-boat racing, horse riding, surfing, guitar playing and motor racing, was even willing to break the taboo on irreverence in an interview with the *Observer*, who quoted him saying: 'It's a game. I don't mean like Monopoly, but a mental exercise.' Such a thought could never be expressed by even a senior manager without incurring all the penalties of a serious breach of taboo. No true-believer in management could bring himself to say it anyway.

The entrepreneur who fails has of course shown himself to be but a mortal who has managed to dupe the gods for a while. In Greek mythology such a character was Tantalus. As a result he was condemned to suffer for eternity, standing up to his neck in water without being able to drink, and with luscious fruits dangling just out of reach over his head. The torment is not unlike that of the entrepreneur who finds himself with a paper fortune which he is unable to turn into cash.

Such people can only expect to pass into myth as warnings of what can happen to those who overreach themselves. The cautionary tales have already begun to weave themselves around John Bloom, for instance, who bought Rolls Razor when its shares were at 2½p in 1960, and took them to 248p at their height with his washing-machine operation, only to see them fade away to nothing in 1964 when he had – the myth says – committed the crime of saturating his market.

Apart from deliberate deception (which, it should be remembered, only becomes deception *after* the failure) there are three main categories of heroes-who-are-punished in mythology, the distinction lying in their intentions. The best-known examples of each are probably Oedipus, Prometheus and Job.

Oedipus is the archetype of the hero who inadvertently transgresses against the will of the gods, but is nevertheless forced to suffer. I have been unable to locate an equivalent myth in management. But it does seem possible that one may build up around the unhappy fate of the Penn-Central conglomerate. Its management tried to do what all good corporate managements are (or were) supposed to do. They diversified out of their declining basic industry into new growth fields, and even maintained abundant sacrifices to the gods in the form of large dividends. While the U S Interstate Commerce Commission has stigmatized its accounting as 'imaginative' – and imagination, while it may be a good quality in managers, is as taboo for an accountant as concupiscence for a Catholic priest or a Vestal virgin – it doesn't seem to have done anything notably different from less thoroughly punished competitors. Except to make those unnecessarily large sacrifices to the gods. In 1967, 1968 and 1969 the two firms – they merged in early 1968 – paid out a total of $153·8 million, while suffering a combined loss of $118 million. To be driven into bankruptcy by paying too much attention to placatory rites may not be as dramatic a fate as that that befell Oedipus, but there are certain parallels. And one feels that the Penn-Central board, like Oedipus, may well have some reason to feel that they have been rather hard done by at the hands of the supernatural powers involved.

For Prometheus it is a little easier to find equivalents. Prometheus deliberately defied the gods in order to help mankind by bringing down some of the divine fire from Olympus which had been forbidden to men. In the end Zeus chained him to a peak in the Caucasus where he had his liver eaten away every day by a vulture. (It grew again every night.) Punishments of that kind are of course no longer possible. Apart from that the story has a certain resemblance to that of Bernie Cornfeld and I O S.

Cornfeld asked his salesmen: 'Do you sincerely want to be rich?' He set out to make them so. He also set out to give investors all over the world the opportunity to do things that were denied them, just as mankind was denied fire by Zeus. To do so he had to defy the most powerful of the supernatural powers in the management cosmology, the international financial establishment. He also defied the governments of several countries, which must be ranked among the supernatural forces, though they are less feared than financiers.

According to the myth Cornfeld couldn't hope to get away with it for long. Ultimately the supernatural powers gathered themselves together and cast him down.

Job's story barely needs retelling. He exemplifies the individual who does everything he should, complies with all the rituals and taboos, and still gets punished. Stories of such figures in management are legion, and like the tale of Job himself, they are used as rationalizations of the fact that it is possible to do all the right things and still fail. The Edsel myth I quoted earlier is of this kind. But in looking for an equivalent figure to Job I cannot at the moment do better than select Lord Stokes. Like Job, Lord Stokes was once a prosperous and respected figure. In 1968 *Management Today* could write: 'The problem of achieving the full benefits of rationalization after a merger, of course, are well-known. Until the arrival of Arnold Weinstock at A E I and Sir Donald Stokes at British Leyland, there were not many examples of swift and urgent action.' To be coupled with the established hero-figure of Arnold Weinstock is an exceptional mark of esteem. However, in early 1971 the *Sunday Times* which had at one time been as fulsome in its praise as anyone could write: 'Three years after the merger the group has only just started to cut back on the wage bill and to trim its assets'. For the Press to switch from attribution of executive *mana* ('swift and urgent') to the implication of taboo-breaking indolence ('Three years after ... has only just started ...') implies a poor profit record, which British Leyland indisputably had in the years that followed its formation. But as far as anyone can see Lord Stokes did everything that a manager is supposed to do, including reorganization, rationalization, and cost reduction, and giving people a car, in the Austin Maxi, they all said they wanted. That all this should result in a declining market share and low profits is, on the face of it, unjust, as were the plagues that afflicted Job.

Lord Stokes, as a professional manager rather than an entrepreneur, is of course, at the moment anyway, not in the running for demigod status. But the central heroes of myth do not necessarily have to be divine. They can as easily be mortal. And this happens to be true of the central figure of the mythological cycle which is probably, for full understanding of the management culture, the most important of all. I have reserved it for special treatment in the next chapter.

14. The Fisher-King

Here is no water but only rock
Rock and no water and the sandy road
The road winding above among the mountains
Which are mountains of rock without water
If there were water we should stop and drink
Amongst the rock one cannot stop or think
Sweat is dry and feet are in the sand
If there were only water amongst the rock
Dead mountain mouth of carious teeth that
   cannot spit
Here one can neither stand nor lie nor sit
There is not even silence in the mountains
But dry sterile thunder without rain
There is not even solitude in the mountains
But red sullen faces sneer and snarl
From doors of mudcracked houses

Well should Lorgres be named with tears,
With bitter weeping, grief and fears.
For here no fertile seed is sown,
Neither peas nor grain are grown,
Never a child of man is born,
Mateless maidens sadly mourn,
On the trees no leaf is seen
Nor are the meadows growing green,
Birds build no nests, no song is sung,
And hapless beasts shall bear no young.

The first of these quotations is from T. S. Eliot. The second is a translation, quoted by Jessie L. Weston, of part of the medieval *Sone de Nansai*. Both poets are describing the same scene – the Waste Land that surrounds the chapel of the Holy Grail.

Once it was fertile. Now it is barren because the king that rules over it is maimed – physically in most versions, spiritually in the *Sone de Nansai*. Not till the king is cured with the coming of a hero will the land be restored. In most of the stories the maimed king bears the title of Fisher. Later in his poem Eliot writes:

> I sat on the shore
> Fishing, with the arid plain behind me

But the Fish is symbolic – symbolic, as it almost always is in folklore, of life. The title merely underlines the belief that the life of the land is dependent upon that of its king.

This belief is widespread, especially in the religions from which our own culture springs – those of the Indo-European and Semitic races. It has three variations. In the story of the Fisher-King the fertility of the land is linked directly to the virility of the human king himself. In the legend of the King of Nemi, which inspired Frazer in *The Golden Bough*, the king personifies a god, and his health is vital to the health of the land. In the third, and most sophisticated, variation the god himself is wounded or dies, and must be restored to full life before the land can quicken again. In this form – in the worship of the god known to the Greeks as Adonis, to the Phrygians as Attis, to the Egyptians as Osiris, and to the Babylonians as Tammuz – it became probably the most widespread cult of all in the classical Mediterranean civilization.

In its simplest and most primitive form the belief reappears in modern management.

For no one in management or around it appears to be in any doubt that the welfare of the company depends absolutely on the virility of its boss. Such virility must be seen in a wider sense than the 'masculine' mental powers of clear-thinking and decisiveness, which I defined as managerial virility in Chapter 10. Almost as important are pure physical health and vigour. Unless the chief executive is, or can be characterized as, 'vigorous', 'youthful', 'logical', 'decisive', 'courageous' and 'determined' a company cannot be successful. That's popular belief.

It is very difficult to challenge. In the first place, it is self-fulfilling. If the chief executive is, or is believed to be, seriously disabled on any of these counts, then two sets of people will lose faith in the future prosperity of the company. One set is the investing public – its present and its potential shareholders. The other set is its staff. A failure in confidence on the part of either set can immediately and directly affect the company's performance, *thereby proving that their belief was right*. All that is in fact proved is that *belief* in the boss's virility affects performance. Whether his true virility has any such effect is another matter.

The popular belief is difficult to challenge for another reason. Success is held to prove virility. This result is then used to justify the general assertion that success depends on virility. It is the circular thinking of the schoolboy's: 'Assume A B C is a straight line; then two angles A B O and C B O add up to 180°. If those angles add up to 180°, then A B C must be a straight line. Therefore A B C is a straight line.' We came across a similar instance in the story about the 'market-oriented' success of the Beecham Group.

It is a *circulum vitiosum,* an empty circle – the argument assumes the conclusion is true, and proves it on that basis. It's rarely easy to get the schoolboy to see that it isn't valid, but with him at least one can fall back on the pragmatic threat that the G C E examiners won't accept it. It's just as difficult to get managers – and some of the people who write about management – to see it, and there is no such enlightened body of assessors in the background.

It is, naturally, one of the basic ways in which magico-religious creeds are justified. In our present context it works something like this. You point to someone who is an obvious exception to the rule, like Jay Hopkins of General Dynamics, who was demonstrably dying while his company was still successful, or Sir John Ellerman or Paul Getty, who are demonstrably aged. The answer you get is, 'Yes, but the *drive* was (or is) still there.' It sounds convincing, but it has neither logical nor empirical validity. The logical validity doesn't really matter. The empirical validity does. It won't have that until it is possible for someone to pick on a chief executive and say: 'He lacks virility – his company is going to get into trouble.' Or 'He's virile – his company's going to do well.' And be consistently correct.

At the moment no one can do that.

On several occasions in their book *The Management of Innovation*, Burns and Stalker come close to some of the major themes of this book, though without making the final step of abandoning the belief that man's behaviour must be rationally motivated. Thus they come across the point I am now dealing with: 'The one constant element of all the studies of the twenty concerns was the extraordinary importance ascribed to the personal qualities of the managing director or general manager of the plant. In many firms, almost every interview would contain reference to the "outstanding personality", the "flair", the "wisdom", the "tremendous personal courage", even the "genius" of the managing director, and the all-important part he had played in the success of the firm.'

Note that nearly all the 'twenty concerns' were involved in the electronics industry. Consequently, a lot of the people being questioned were scientists, engineers, and technicians, whom one would normally expect to take a pragmatic view of life. Note too the use of the word 'extraordinary' to describe a phenomenon which is at the same time 'the one constant element'. On the basis of my thesis the phenomenon would not only be ordinary, but predictable.

Coming even closer to the heart of the matter, the authors go on to say: '... even if it is granted that such remarks were merely a precaution or a propitiatory ritual, they exemplify with sufficient force the pervasiveness of the influence cast by the managing director over the conduct of the members of the concern ... The head of the concern stands for the concern and its relative successes – he symbolizes or personifies it.'

The true point is narrowly missed. Such remarks *are* a ritual, but not a propitiatory one. They are expressive. The manager makes the assertions because he needs to believe they are true for the sake of his own security. Otherwise the company is doomed to failure. If the king is not whole and potent, the land is laid waste.

Essentially the same belief is held by the investing public. Perhaps the simplest evidence is given by the immense majority of proxy forms that are automatically returned by shareholders, endorsed in favour of the chairman. (The reciprocity of belief is interesting. The manager ascribes supernatural power to the shareholder. In return the shareholder believes in the supernatural power of the manager.) But there is other evidence. Anybody who has made an attempt to raise money for a new project will know it. What counts more than anything else is the *mana* of the manager responsible. It is even more important than the glamour (in good times) or the security (in bad ones) of the industry concerned. It is certainly more important than the figures and the analyses.

No matter how carefully calculated, exhaustively analysed, and voluminously documented, a project presented by someone without the requisite magical attributes invites rejection. But the same project presented by a man with an established reputation for executive virility is likely to be accepted if it is, figuratively speaking, written on the back on an envelope. Similarly, in the typical proxy battle or disputed takeover the relative potency of the individuals concerned will count for far more than the elaborately presented written arguments. With small shareholders this may be partly because they do not understand the written arguments, and with institutional shareholders because they are sophisticated enough to distrust such calculations. But in both cases it is ultimately belief in the myth of the Fisher-King that tells.

The Press has a complex part to play in all this. Both the popular and the specialist Press are firm believers in the myth. Automatically, photographs of chief executives accompany – discreetly or rampantly, according to the publication – stories and articles about their companies, even if they are factually so irrelevant that the chief executives are not mentioned in the text. Regular columns, like *Fortune*'s 'Businessmen in the News', help to institutionalize the belief that what matters is the personality.

The bosses of successful companies are inexorably described as being 'firm', 'youthful', 'decisive', 'determined to call the tune'. With equal predictability the heads of failed or unexciting companies are called 'staid', 'ageing', 'long serving'. Thus the Press also plays its part in perpetuating the self-justification of the myth. Finally, it plays an essential part in the propagation of the individual reputation. Adulatory or derogatory comment in print is more important in determining the valuation placed on an individual, and therefore on his company, than the facts of its record or present situation.

Television is in a rather different situation. In its news and comment programmes it tends to play much the same role as the Press. But it is a strong encourager of heresy when it manages to tempt business leaders to appear in person. For it is impossible to distinguish the leaders of successful businesses from those of the stagnant. Just as it is in real life.

Under the unlikely face of Lord Beeching, then wielding his 'axe' (a potent virility symbol) on British Railways, the *Sunday Times* could write: 'In a room filled with maps of the doomed railways, the doctor controls their extinction as firmly as he proposed it.' The paper managed to convey an impression of ruthless determination tinged with wizardry. When Lord Beeching appeared on television, it was a little difficult to maintain the picture, or to endow him with any outstanding characteristics at all. Since the fate of the 'doomed' railways was ultimately to be decided by a piecemeal process of compromise between disputatious pressure groups, it seems likely that the television picture was the truer one.

But, as I have pointed out, magical beliefs are above factual refutation. The truth revealed by television's face-to-face interviews is overshadowed by the fictions of its big-business plays and serials. Not, as Burns and Stalker might have felt, in an extraordinary way, but predictably. After all, the myth has at least four thousand years of history behind it.

As a final reinforcement of the argument, let me tell a tale that is now firmly part of the mythology of management, at least in Britain. Though not quite in the way I tell it.

Once upon a time there was a king. In his youth he had been a mighty warrior and a wise ruler. His kingdom had grown and prospered. His people had been rich and proud. But he had grown old, and his courtiers and barons had grown grey alongside him. As a result, his kingdom had fallen into desolation and neighbouring kings had stolen parts of it for themselves.

Nevertheless, as yet his lands were wide. Many people believed them to be still fertile. They believed that only the king's dotage caused its barrenness. And so, one day, there arrived at

the king's court a message from a great magician, who had
used his secret powers to build himself a kingdom out of nothing. The message demanded that the old king give up his realm
or be prepared to do battle for it.

The old king and his courtiers knew their powers were declining. The contemptuous demand was, however, too much
for their dignity to accept. They prepared themselves for battle,
but their hearts were low. Although they knew that their
people loved the old king for what he had given them in the
past, they also knew that most of them were sorely tempted by
the magician's promises of riches.

Then one day a young prince rode up to the king's castle.
He was richly dressed and powerful. He came from a faraway
land where his father had also been a king. When his father
died, the prince had ascended to the throne, pacified his kingdom, and restored its fortunes. But he had made a vow to seek
out new lands and new riches, and to build for himself an
empire that men everywhere would know and respect and fear,
as they had the emperors of old. He offered the old king a
treaty: he would do battle against the magician in his stead,
but in return he must be given half the kingdom and the
stewardship of the rest. As the prince was young and strong,
and as he had fought many battles which had made him famous around the world, the old king agreed.

When the day of battle came, the young prince was loved by
all who saw him, by gods as well as men, and his magic was
too powerful for the sorcerer-king who left the field uttering
dire warnings. But from that day forward his magic powers
deserted him, and before the year was past he even lost his
own kingdom. The prince however took over the stewardship
of the old king's realm, made it prosper, and conquered other
countries as he pursued his dream of empire.

This kind of story is common in the mythology of many
lands. Only the names change. But for the young prince read
Rupert Murdoch, for the sorcerer Robert Maxwell, for the old
king Sir William Carr, and for his kingdom the *News of the
World*. It then is a reasonably accurate account of the way in
which the story of the Australian's arrival in London was told
in the Press and has subsequently been enshrined in the mem-

ories of those who watched it happen. The great thing about the story as a myth is that its essentials are more or less true. It can therefore be quoted as evidence in a way that was not possible with the myths of Gawain or Galahad.

The myth does overlook some facts though. There is no evidence really for any causal connection between the relative age of the participants and their powers. The *News of the World* isn't demonstrably better off since the famous battle. And even should it be restored to runaway success its sensitivity to public taste compared to its rivals' is more likely to be the reason than the virility of their bosses.

Any attempt to construct a myth of the same sort around, for instance, the *Sunday Telegraph* would be doomed to fail. It is now doing marginally better than when it was launched. But its management is ten years older. Stories only have the stuff of myth when they conform to popular superstition.

A belief that the health of the land depends on the health and vitality of its king has a natural consequence. When the king is obviously failing, something has to be done about it. The simplest thing is to find a new king. There is a persuasive simplicity about the idea that the best way to do that is to have the new man challenge and beat the old king in some kind of contest. It is the major theme of the most famous of all collections of anthropological data, Sir James Frazer's *The Golden Bough*.

Frazer set out to discover why, in classical times, in a grove sacred to Diana on the shores of the Lake of Nemi in the Alban Hills, the priest, known as the King of the Wood, reigned until a fugitive slave managed to take a branch from a tree in the wood, and kill him with it. The slave then took the title, and reigned till he was dispossessed in his turn. Frazer's search for an answer took him through a total of thirteen volumes, spread over nearly half a century (inspiring along the way T. S. Eliot and Miss Weston, and therefore both the quotations that opened this chapter). Ultimately he believed himself to have shown that the probable explanation – he insisted on the 'probable' – was that outlined above: the King of the Wood was a relic of one of the sacred kings of antiquity who were linked with the fertility of the land, and who therefore had to be ritually slain by their successor as soon as their physical powers demonstrably weakened.

Frazer has been criticized on many grounds. Perhaps he did go too far in postulating that this was a developmental stage through which all cultures *must* pass. There is plenty of evidence however that it is a stage through which some cultures *did* go. Thus in the early years of this century, the local District Commissioner reported of the Ju-Ju of Elele in southern Nigeria, a priest-king elected for a seven-year term: 'The whole prosperity of the town, especially the fruitfulness of farm, byre and marriage-bed, was linked with his life. Should he fall sick it entailed famine and grave disaster upon the inhabitants.' As soon as a successor was elected, the Ju-Ju was said to 'die for himself'. Before colonial rule he could be put to death and succeeded by any man who was strong enough.

In the twentieth-century management culture, of course, the kings are not killed. As I have noted before, the parallel of violent death is dismissal. But there is a pervasive trend in the management culture to dismiss a chief executive and replace him by 'a younger man' any time that younger man is powerful enough to bring off the required boardroom coup. Such a coup will be considered right and natural whatever the current state of the company. It will in any case be hailed by the Press as a harbinger of improvement. But it will be especially supported when either the chief executive is visibly departing from the established standard of managerial vitality, or the company is doing so badly that the powers of the chief executive are believed to be failing. At such a time the challenger will have less personal fear of retribution. He will gain support from elders whose own personal security is bound up with the prosperity of the company. He can also count on help from any supernatural forces that may take an interest. Sometimes indeed the initial motivation for the challenge may come from the elders, or from outside forces. They are unlikely though to take any such action unless they have at hand a champion with the required characteristics. Otherwise a solution is more likely to be found in annexation of the company by another headed by a man still in demonstrable possession of his *mana*.

Dispossession of this kind has happened many times in

many places, though frequently the dismissal is cloaked as a voluntary retirement (which equals natural death). It just so happens that one of the examples with which I am best acquainted also happens to be one of the clearest instances of the entire cycle at work. It is the story I promised to return to when I wrote in the Introduction of the ritual purification that took place in Cecil King's suite of offices after his dismissal as chairman of the International Publishing Corporation. The central figure of the story is, by some streak of coincidence, most appropriately named.

I P C was formed in 1963 in an operation to tidy up the complex of companies belonging to the Daily Mirror Group. In popular language, both inside and outside the company, it continued to be referred to by that name, and the fortunes of the *Daily Mirror* continued to dominate the group quite as thoroughly as those of Rome did the classical Roman Empire. The history of I P C is as much part of the history of the *Daily Mirror* as the history of the British Empire is part of the history of England.

The story therefore starts many years earlier, when the Daily Mirror Group was little more than the *Mirror* itself and its companion, the *Sunday Pictorial*. Alone among major British newspapers at the time, it was not owner-controlled. Daily Mirror Newspapers Ltd held a majority of the shares of Sunday Pictorial Newspapers Ltd. Reciprocally the *Sunday Pictorial* was the major shareholder in the *Mirror*. Both companies were controlled by essentially the same board, none of whom had significant shareholdings in either company. The chairman was Henry Guy Bartholomew. In 1951 he had held the office for just under a decade and was, significantly, almost seventy years old.

The subsequent story has been told several times, notably in the semi-official *The Mirror: A political history* by Maurice Edelman. Edelman's language is significant. Its linkage with the King of the Wood mythology is evident. 'Bartholomew's dogmatism,' he writes, 'had increased as his touch became less sure ... There had been growing dissatisfaction on the Mirror board with his hectoring manner and a developing misanthropy which drink didn't relieve.' Luckily the con-

cerned board had a fresh and relatively young champion at
hand in Cecil Harmsworth King. He was only just fifty and a
physically impressive six feet four inches tall. (I stick to the
tradition by which King is never referred to without mention-
ing his physical size.) Edelman reports a lunch between King
and Philip Zec, another director, as the challenge got under
way. Again the language is significant: 'There King told him
that together with Sylvester Bolam, the editor and a close
friend and dependant of Bartholomew, he had come to the
conclusion that Bartholomew, now *nearly seventy*, was *in his
dotage* and *had to be* disposed of. Zec himself had suggested to
Bartholomew six months previously that he ought to resign
since, as a colleague put it, "the *old man* was *drinking too
much* and had become *incoherent* and *unreliable*".' The italics
are mine. They indicate a condemnation as thorough-going as
suggesting that the Ju-Ju of Elele had become impotent.

The result was inevitable. The vigorous King replaced the
ailing Bartholomew on a majority board vote. With an un-
consciously revealing simile, Edelman continues the story:
'For the next four days, Zec had the unhappy task of persuading Bartholomew to write the four necessary letters of resignation. It was rather *like persuading a man under sentence of
death to write his will* when he couldn't believe that the sentence had been pronounced.'

By the time I joined I P C this story had passed into myth,
as had several tales of the subsequent heroic exploits of King
in building up his empire. His accession had been justified by
his conquest of his predecessor. His subsequent retention of
the chair had to be legitimized by tales of his determination, his
omniscience, his puritanism, his foresight. Factually, the
growth curves of the *Daily Mirror* and *Sunday Pictorial* display no sudden change of direction in 1951. They continued to
expand and prosper, but no more so than the *Express* and the
Telegraph, both under the control of contemporaries of Bartholomew. (Neither Lord Beaverbrook nor Lord Camrose gave
up the reins until they died. Under Beaverbrook's son the *Express* faded dramatically, while under Camrose's sons the
Telegraph continued much as before. As Kurt Vonnegut's
Tralfamadorians would say, so it goes.)

Nevertheless Edelman, writing in 1966, goes on to say: 'Whereas Bartholomew had developed the Daily Mirror and Sunday Pictorial companies in a series of commercial impulses, some of which ... brought disappointment and failure, King, a new type of businessman-intellectual, *planned* his newspaper expansion by entering profitable fields hitherto unploughed by his organization.'

If he was a 'new type of businessman' it was a type that believed expansion meant buying rival companies, changing the chairmen and leaving them to continue their rivalries. If he 'planned' the expansion, it was without the knowledge of the executives one might have expected to share in those plans. His final acquisition, of the legal and professional publishers Butterworth & Co., was a reflex action motivated by a dislike of seeing it bought either by American bidders or Robert Maxwell. Subsequently, Butterworth's pre-tax profits just about repaid the interest on the loan stock with which it was bought. It was never integrated into the rest of the organization.

Similarly, his first major acquisition, Amalgamated Press in 1959, happened because its then owners, Lord Kemsley and the late Lord Camrose's sons, wanted to sell. As his deputy Hugh Cudlipp made clear in *At Your Peril*, King's impulse to buy was based more on the desire to take over the company which had been the foundation of the empire of his famous and admired uncle than on any vague ideas that women's magazines were a good field for expansion.

However, in the mid-sixties, the myths were still believed and fostered by books like Edelman's and Cudlipp's. Aloofly conscious of his own power, King strictly observed all the appropriate taboos. A Behavioural Scientist or sophisticated organization theorist might have objected to his managerial attitudes. They were typified by his habit of appearing briefly at staff conferences, swiftly and disdainfully reading through prepared speeches, and then disappearing. On one occasion he stopped, turned back a page, said, 'Whatever that may have meant', and carried on. But more orthodox believers noted all the accepted attributes of management virility, despite the fact that he was 'nearly seventy'.

Unfortunately, all was not well. As Anthony Hilton was to

write in the *Observer*: 'It was also a totally unco-ordinated empire. Communications between the different divisions were virtually non-existent; different sections employed different accounting principles; and there was no co-ordination of selling techniques. I P C was not, and still is not, a cohesive unit.' It showed in the profits which went into steep decline after peaking in 1966. It showed in the share price which did the same. The land was demonstrably waste. The need for a regenerative ritual was apparent.

It needed a champion, and an occasion. The champion was somewhat reluctantly to hand in the deputy chairman, Hugh Cudlipp. He was in his early fifties and a suitable personification of physical vigour and decisiveness. In 1964 the *Sunday Times* had even described him as 'boyish' when he had presided over 'the biggest and boldest newspaper venture of the century', the launch of the *Sun* newspaper. In suitably entrepreneurial fashion he was quoted as saying: 'You don't think I'd take all these risks and leave it to somebody else, do you?' In fact by 1968 the *Sun* was an evident dreary flop, but nevertheless Cudlipp was the only acceptable challenger. (Paul Hamlyn, the self-made millionaire whom Cecil King had bought into the group, had fractured far too many managerial taboos; so, in different ways, had the equally egregious Arnold Quick, the only other member of the board with demonstrated entrepreneurial success behind him.)

The occasion came in February of 1968 at a conference optimistically entitled 'I P C '73'. The senior management of the corporation was supposed to review the achievements of its first five years and to lay the foundations of its plans for the next five. Typically, King was present for only one evening of the three-day conference. His speech had been written in two halves by different members of his staff. One was about the state of the country. The other dealt with the state of I P C. That it was read as rapidly and expressionlessly as usual shows even on the tape-recording; but in deference to the seniority of the conference members King consented to answer questions. (Cudlipp and the managing director Frank Rogers were both present, and so ominously enough was Don Ryder, managing director of the Reed Group and a non-executive director of I P C.) It was painfully apparent to everyone listening that, whatever his past planning had been like, his thinking for the future was restricted to an intuitive feeling that the only growth opportunity in publishing was provided by books, and that in no circumstances could I P C ever be taken over.

Such was his spell however that it took an outsider to break it. At lunch the following day he was invited to give his impressions of the conference. He started favourably, until he reached Wednesday evening when 'the old man' came along. He stopped. He apologized, explaining that in America the term 'old man' in this context meant no disrespect, but was merely the usual colloquial term for the boss. 'So,' he restarted, 'along came this old old man ...' The laughter was at first tentative, then prolonged. King's spell had been broken. Once he had denounced Bartholomew as 'in his dotage'. Now he himself was an 'old old man'. As the conference ended, in a blaze of fraternal feeling never equalled before or after in I P C, Cudlipp knew that whatever support he needed would be forthcoming.

The coup could not be long delayed. It happened, to King's astonishment, in May. The details are unimportant, beside the fact that once again the drama of the King of the Wood had played itself out.

On any other basis the coup is difficult to explain. As a straightforward piece of power-gaming, it doesn't stand up. Both Cudlipp and Rogers had been protégés of King. Both still displayed immense respect for him. Both were in the direct line of succession to the chairmanship. Cudlipp had been nominated by King, and Rogers was nearly a decade younger than Cudlipp. Neither of them was sufficiently driven by personal ambition to do it on those grounds.

Nor is it a simple example of a straightforward substitution of a better man. There was no reason to suspect that Cudlipp would make a better chief executive than King. In fact there was every reason to suspect that he would be worse. A talented editor himself – perhaps even, as has been said, a genius – he had always made it plain that he was somehow above management. In one speech at least he referred openly to the need for editorial and management to go ahead hand in hand – but with management two steps behind. Nothing could have been more calculated to intensify the emotional antagonism that already divided the two camps in I P C. Nothing could have been more necessary than to break it down.

The record speaks for itself. The substitution of Cudlipp for King put no halt to I P C's decline.

There is every evidence that Cudlipp was aware of his own deficiency as a manager. Coupling this with his own feeling for King, the only explanation for his action, as well as his support, is that he had been trapped by the mythology that preaches the need for a new king to expel the old once his potency declines.

Ironically, less than two years later he was to approach the Reed Group whose chairman Don Ryder had heard Cecil King's speech at I P C '73, and subsequently replaced him as chairman at the same time that Cudlipp took over at I P C, for a merger, with the admitted aim of obtaining an 'injection of fresh managerial talent'. It became immediately obvious that the major site for the new injection would be at the top. Ryder, almost a stereotype of the virile executive, became chairman of both companies, to the acclaim of everyone but a small number of the I P C staff who attempted to fight the merger with a sort of Jacobite futility. The romance of their position attracted some emotional support and wide Press coverage, but had little practical effect.

It's worth noting some of the Press characterizations of Ryder at the time. He was 'firmly in the saddle' (*Guardian*), 'Reed personified ... intensely ambitious' (*Daily Telegraph*), 'the archetypal hard-faced, hard-playing, hard-working, un-compromising professional' (*Sunday Times*), 'active and ruthless ... straightforward ... a real businessman' (*Observer*). To the *Evening Standard* reporter who detailed his strenuous, eighteen-hour working day, he asserted : 'A lunch that is not a working lunch is a waste of time'.

The factual record was, as usual, more ambiguous. Reed had grown enormously by take-over since Ryder became managing director. But by most normal criteria – return on assets, on capital employed, margin on turnover – its profitability was then lower than I P C's, and the steady growth in absolute profits had been accompanied by a steady decline in earnings per share.

It didn't matter. Once more the search for the magical powers of a potent king had been concluded. This time the king had abdicated, and his successor had come from another country. The essential point of the ritual had been the same.

As it almost always is, almost everywhere. The need of an ailing company is always diagnosed as 'new, vital, dynamic, youthful' management. The new king does not always have to dispossess his successor. Lord Kearton won the right to the chairmanship of Courtauld's by the power with which he fought against the giant I C I attempting to take over his country, much as Theseus won the right to the throne of Athens. But there has to be a new king. And no matter how often his succession makes no difference, or even worsens the state of the company, the myth continues to survive. It is one of 'the beliefs that cannot be destroyed by the presentation of contrary evidence'.

Conclusion

An American business magazine once spent some time analysing the managerial styles and practices of the ten most successful major corporations. At the end it admitted, rather apologetically, that it had found no common factor between them. There were decentralized companies, centralized companies, autocratic companies, democratic companies, companies with formal planning functions, companies without them. Reviews of this kind are always producing similar uncomfortable facts. I have already quoted Joan Woodward's work in Essex and *Fortune*'s judgement on the mutual fund managements, and these are only two of many.

By now one would have thought that the truth would have been accepted. There is no more likelihood of finding practices that are uniquely linked with success than there is of finding common ground in the approaches of the world's ten most successful rain-makers. The evidence is all around us, yet it remains ignored. Managers everywhere still cling to the belief that there are formulae, principles, practices that will ensure success.

Sometimes they think they have found them. Obviously this faith tends to be more common in successful companies, but it is not restricted to them. Managers in declining companies still behave as they always have, in the pious belief that the rituals of their golden age still retain their potency. I remember the shiver of familiarity I felt when reading Ruth Benedict's description of a Digger Indian chief: 'When he talked of the shamans who had transformed themselves into bears before his eyes in the bear dance, his hands trembled and his voice broke with excitement. It was an incomparable thing, the power his people had had in the old days.'

More often the manager believes that the really efficacious technique is still around the corner. Somewhere – in work study, in industrial engineering, in Behavioural Science, in autonomous systems, in decentralization, in planned management development, in one of a hundred other fashionable phrases – he must be able to find the true secret. And so he reads success stories, listens to successful speakers, analyses case studies, attends conferences and seminars. Not always is he credulous, frequently he is cynical. But even where the cynicism is not simply a cloak to cover confusion or a refusal to admit lack of understanding, it is normally only the result of an inner belief that he himself already knows the real truth.

There is really no better argument for my basic thesis than the existence of this pattern of behaviour despite all empirical evidence. It conjures up two pictures. One is of the medieval alchemists intent on their search for the Philosopher's Stone, with its magic power to turn base metals into gold. The other is of the addicts who cluster around roulette tables, obsessed with the attempt to discover the system that will ensure they make their fortunes.

Both groups are as doomed to fail as the seekers after an infallible guide to business success. But the second analogy is slightly better. For the alchemists had nothing to buoy up their hopes but their beliefs. Unfortunately for their sense of objectivity the roulette-players, like the managers, have the occasional visible evidence of success. Some roulette players are bound to win, even among those who play systems. And each example of a successful player provides the kernel for the building of fresh legends to sustain the hopes of the addicts.

Similarly, some businesses are bound to succeed. Our society and our economy are structured that way. And every company that succeeds, every entrepreneur that makes a fortune, provides further evidence for the belief that there must be a road to success, even if it is only the road of hard work and long hours. This, more than anything, is the pathetic fallacy of the managerial society.

It is a fallacy that I can't quite bring myself to discard completely any more than I can wholly share it. The evidence is that our cherished practices and beliefs are simply magical rituals and religious dogma that we evolve to protect ourselves from uncertainty. But, strictly speaking, there is no evidence that it will always be so. Nor is there evidence that all of our practices are solely ritualistic, or that rituals themselves are necessarily a waste of time.

Out of alchemy came a soundly based science of chemistry and physics. Out of the perennial fascination of gambling came a mathematics of probability that eventually helped us to control the atom and the electron. It is at least possible to hope that out of the present welter of logical rationalizations, sanctified dogma, and automatic rituals there will one day emerge something like a science of management. And, on this basis, a technology of management that will have the minimal virtue of being able to predict the results of its actions.

At the moment we are a long way from that ideal. And we may well have to wait until both economics and psychology have established rather more solid scientific and technological grounds for us to walk on. In the meantime there are a few things that we can do which may help a little, even though they will never lead us to a managerial Philosopher's Stone.

In the first place we can use the insights that anthropological study can give to help in understanding and affecting the behaviour of people around us. (I use the word 'anthropology' in its broadest possible sense – the unfashionable nineteenth-century concept of a 'science of man'.) I do not pretend to know how people ought to behave to achieve success in management any more than I claim to know how they should behave in order to achieve eternal salvation. But any manager will want at some time to change the behaviour of his subordinates. He is also likely to want to change the behaviour of his colleagues and superiors. And about that particular process I do claim to have learned a little.

Not that I intend to preach any particular techniques. Given my choice of weapons, I think I would usually pick drugs and hypnosis, but they tend to be ruled out in normal managerial circumstances. But there are a few necessary ground-rules. The basic one is to recognize that people are not rational creatures. Their behaviour is not rationally motivated, even if it can be rationally 'explained'.

It is of little use therefore to attempt to change anyone's behaviour by rational argument. It may be possible to convince

him that what he believes is wrong, and that what he does is
silly. But it will merely change his verbal behaviour. In future
he will apologize for what he has done, but he will still do it.
His present behaviour pattern is almost certainly the complex
result of his own attempts to assert his own individuality while
at the same time demonstrating his membership of a community. It will also be shaped by the conditioning he has received since childhood and is still receiving from the continual
pressures of the rewards and punishments that his environment provides. I mean not just the major ones that stick in the
memory or that are deliberately given. The tiny ones – the
raised eyebrows, the marks of inattention, the unexpected
smiles – are all the time exerting their own pressures. And at
bottom there is likely to be a congenital bias that nothing, except possibly drug therapy, is ever going to change.

With all that going on it's hardly surprising that argument
doesn't get very far. Conditioning on the other hand can produce results, given time. But it implies two things – control of
the environment and an understanding of what the individual
sees as reward and punishment. The degree to which the manager controls the environment of the people he manages varies.
It is never better than limited. But in so far as he can affect the
situation he needs to make sure that the behaviour he wants to
see is rewarded, and anything else is punished. A company that
wants, for instance, to get its managers to adopt Renée Likert's 'System 4' managerial style, spends money and time on
convincing them that 'System 4' is the right system, and then
continues to reward 'System 1' and punish anything else, is
going to continue to have 'System 1' managers. That should be
self-evident. But there are an awful lot of companies that do
just that.

It is essential that the rewards and punishments are recognized (behaviourally, not verbally) as rewards and punishments. About the only safe thing there is to say about such
'motivating factors', even without going into the excesses of
masochism, is that very few people are alike. It is fatal to
assume that anyone else responds to the same things as oneself
– or that there are particular things that people 'ought to' be
grateful for.

Let us assume, however, that the manager is paying careful attention to his reward systems. He objectively assesses what the reward factors in his particular circumstances are. Conditioning can still fail. It will do so if the desired behaviour pattern does not offer the same opportunities for emotional release as the old one. Otherwise the new reward system and the old emotional impulses will interact to produce a behaviour pattern which may be new but won't be the one intended.

If one expressive ritual is abolished, another must be substituted. I came across a company once in which virtually all the operating decisions were taken at low level, but they required approval from higher up. As part of a drive to 'increase delegation', the formal requirements for approval were lifted. Managers were now free to take the decisions that they had been making anyway. The result was not an increase in the speed of decision-making, but the opposite. Managers who had confidently submitted requests for approval now dithered before 'making decisions'. Where they didn't simply dither they investigated, analysed, commissioned reports – invented, in fact, new rituals to replace the old one of which they had been deprived.

The referring of decisions higher up the hierarchy was undoubtedly from a rational point of view a waste of time. But that didn't mean it should be eliminated. People need rituals. The art, if there is one, is to design rituals that produce only a minimal drag on efficiency.

They are most likely to need them in association with the decision-making process. When a manager makes a decision he is at his most vulnerable. I suspect many attempts at decentralization of decision-making fail because they do not make allowance for such needs. Certainly most of the preaching in favour of delegation of decisions ignores the fact that it increases the pressures of insecurity on the people who are supposedly being rewarded by 'increased participation'.

How the relative rewards and punishments balance out depends entirely on the emotional make-up of the person involved. From watching what has happened in a variety of situations it seems likely that the protagonists of delegation have assumed too readily that their own personal biases were

widely shared. Durkheim coined the term 'anomie' to describe
the withdrawal and inertia of people confronted by their
powerlessness in the face of the organization. It differs very
little from the state observable in many companies where individuals have been confronted by their powerlessness in face of
the responsibility for making decisions. (Not of course that any
manager can admit to such an obvious lack of executive
mana.)

To change the behaviour of such individuals is far from
easy. The manager attempting to do it needs all the help he
can get from magical and religious rituals. For the process is
very much akin to religious conversion. Faith can only be conquered by a counter-faith. It is impervious to fact.

The central importance of the hero-figure in management
mythology indicates what effect a sufficiently powerful individual should be able to have on managerial behaviour. Unfortunately it is not a conclusion of any practical use. From
watching the way in which managers will react to a suitably
charismatic leader, it is undoubtedly true that one can produce
desirable changes very quickly. But to say that charisma is a
useful tool isn't to help very much. The charismatic leader
already does use it, and the manager without charisma can't. I
don't know of any way to acquire it except to make a quick
fortune.

I was on a course once where none of the participants
knew each other's backgrounds, not even their companies or
their titles. At the beginning they sat around a table and introduced themselves by giving their names and saying a little
about their personal and domestic lives. Afterwards each member was asked to write down the name of the individual he
would most like to work for. We worked together intensively,
took part in exhaustive analyses of each other's behaviour and
personality, and finally revealed our business backgrounds. It
took a week. We again wrote down the name of the person we
would most like to work for. We also rated each other on a list
of personality traits. Both times the same two individuals had
a majority of votes as desirable bosses, and the ranking on that
score correlated insignificantly with all the personality traits.

One small-scale experiment of that kind of course serves

very little purpose except to confirm one's prejudices if the result agrees with them. Nevertheless I have yet to see any behavioural science doctrine that does anything to explain that result, or the, to me, evident fact that some individuals can command virtually instant respect from others (not by any means everybody).

It is sometimes possible to manipulate such a charismatic figure, even if the manipulator himself lacks charisma. Where such individuals exist in an organization, it can pay to concentrate behavioural-change effort on them, relying on their influence to multiply the effect. Conversely, and even more certainly, to ignore them is virtually to ensure defeat. Their power to induce others to follow their example is greater than that of any of the behavioural techniques at the moment available to the less endowed manager.

Finally, the only other effective inducer of behavioural change is an emotional shock. In a way, it is simply a variant of the conditioning process taken to a condensed and sometimes violent extreme. It consists of suddenly and sharply punishing someone for behaviour that he has hitherto considered good. It is most effective when the individual has been placed in an emotionally vulnerable situation. (Sometimes, but less often, the reverse mechanism occurs – an unexpected reward for something hitherto considered bad.)

The effect of the T-group and its variants is based on this mechanism. The individuals concerned are placed in a situation in which all the normal behavioural taboos have been relaxed. All the normal supportive rituals are removed. Even the man who 'ought' to display the characteristics of executive *mana*, the course leader, steadfastly refuses to do so, thereby removing another prop against insecurity. That creates the desired vulnerability. The individuals are then encouraged to display openly what they feel about each other. To be confronted by open criticism, hostility or rejection is sufficient punishment to a manager used to being cosseted by the complex structure of managerial taboos, and in particular the taboo against direct criticism. The T-group can be an effective method of changing behaviour in an individual. Unfortunately it is difficult to link such lessons to the work environment. The induced behavioural change is more likely to affect his personal life than his managerial behaviour.

There are other ways of creating shock situations which can be valuable, but they all suffer from the same general weakness. They all necessitate the concentration of a great deal of effort on one individual, and are therefore uneconomic unless the particular individual is of exceptional significance. Much the same is true of psychotherapy. The resemblance underlines the fact that the production of behavioural change in an organization is a branch of psychotherapy (except that 'therapy' implies making better, rather than just changing). Therefore it needs to rely on similar techniques. While it may be possible to differentiate between 'normal' and 'pathological' behaviour, it remains true that to change one 'normal' pattern of behaviour to another is just as great a task as to change an 'abnormal' pattern to a 'normal' one.

Recognizing ritual and irrational behaviour for what they are is therefore an important aid to understanding and affecting others. But it can also help to recognize the same things in oneself. Again, that does not mean that we should try to eliminate them, which is probably impossible anyway. It does mean that we are more effective if we understand why we do what we do.

Personally, I cross my fingers if I'm looking for a seat in a crowded train. I frequently carry out paper calculations to eight or nine significant places 'in order to' get the first three right. Like a lot of other things I do, these are meaningless rituals. I don't bother to try and stop them. The first one does no harm, and the second rarely does more than keep me up late. But understanding them for what they are helps a little when for one reason or another I can't carry them out; and I don't try to get other people to do them too.

Another, irrational, article of faith is that we are more effective, if we can come to terms with randomness. A simple question will prove how deeply ingrained it is in us. Can we bring ourselves to face the fact that it is impossible to predict whether a decision is going to be 'right' or not? I am not sure that the concept of correctness can even be applied to decisions in advance. A decision only becomes right or wrong when the predictions on which it is based are tested. It is a trick of language that enables us to talk of wanting to make the 'right' decision. At that particular moment no such thing as a 'right' decision exists.

This is not entirely a linguistic quibble. It has practical results. Once we can face the fact that we cannot be sure of the future, and that therefore we can never 'make the right decision', we can with a little luck divert some of the time, money and energy we spend on trying to find it into planning the contingent action we are going to take when things go wrong. If we cut down on the analyses, investigations and reports, maybe we can get alternative lines of action prepared. Maybe we can then set up more effective monitoring and control systems, and do all the other things that usually get overlooked in the tension of the struggle to make the 'right' choice. Finally, if we aren't so heavily committed to a specific project, maybe we will be readier to change it or even kill it as soon as we get the feed-back that tells us that the decision was in fact 'wrong'.

Maybe we still need to express our tension with rituals. If, however, we understand what we are doing, we can at least choose ones that don't significantly affect our efficiency. Putting one's trust in God has the great merit that it doesn't take long, doesn't cost much, doesn't involve much effort. As an expressive ritual it used to be as effective as market research is now. As a means of ensuring success it had about the same track record.

I'd hate anyone to think that I'm suggesting that all research, all decision analysis, all planning has no pragmatic value. Some of it has. In particular, the planning activity of estimating different outcomes of a decision and inventing different strategies to take account of those different outcomes is crucial. So is the process of making clear the objectives one is *really* trying to achieve. So are many other things. But most of the time we go too far, and, unless we understand why, we are unlikely ever to be objective enough to differentiate between the pragmatically useful and the ritual.

If we then want to keep the ritual, let it stand. If we need its comfort to protect us against the knowledge that forces we do not understand and cannot control will determine whether our decision was right or wrong, whether we succeed or fail, then at least we are displaying our humanity. It demonstrates that we still have something in common with men of all ages and all lands. And that itself is some comfort.

Acknowledgements

Most of the authors whose books I have been indebted to are mentioned in the text. Of them however I would like to single out Professor Lucy Mair's Pelican Original, *Primitive Government,* as being of especial value to any manager concerned with organization planning. Almost as valuable are Jessie L. Weston's discussion of the Fisher-King myths in *From Ritual to Romance* (Cambridge University Press/Doubleday Anchor) and *The Quest of The Holy Grail* originally published by G. Bell & Sons but now available as a reprint by Frank Cass & Co.; both books are in any case worth reading for their own sake. Particularly piquant for anyone bred in the managerial culture is Ruth Benedict's *Patterns of Culture* (Routledge & Kegan Paul): her descriptions of both the paranoiac Dobuan community and the passionless Pueblo Indians are frighteningly familiar.

Angus Downie's description of Sir James Frazer in *Frazer and the Golden Bough* (Gollancz) was of more help than might be readily apparent. *The Golden Bough* itself (Macmillan) is of course worth reading, irrespective of one's other interests, though the two-volume abridgement is rather more manageable than the whole work.

As a first step in anthropological reading I know of nothing better than Professor Mair's *Introduction to Social Anthropology* (OUP), though it has a certain British bias. Her suggestions for further reading are obviously more comprehensive than I could hope to suggest.

On the management side, those of my readers who are managers will already be flooded with books, and those who are not would perhaps rather not know. But anyone who is disappointed (or infuriated) by my cursory treatment of the Hawthorne legend might care to read the full and accurate story in *Management and the Worker* (Harvard): equally, anyone irritated by my treatment of the cyberneticists might care to re-read Stafford Beer's *Decision and Control*, especially the passages dealing with Hegel's Axiom of Internal Relations, and think again. (Having said that, it would be churlish not to acknowledge my debt to several private disputations with Stafford Beer, many of which made me think again.)

I owe a continuing debt to Bertram Gross for writing *The Managing of Organizations* (Macmillan), though it is somewhat marred by his allowing a one-volume abridgement, *Organizations and their Managing*, which concentrates on the practical essence and leaves out the interesting bits. It retains however a few pages on the place of ritual in management which are related to my thesis, and has the most compendious managerial bibliography.

Two chapters in Anthony Jay's *Management and Machiavelli* (Hodder & Stoughton, also Pelican Books) also touch on the same theme; another not irrelevant book is Thurman Arnold's *The Folklore of Capitalism* (Yale), though it is on a somewhat different tangent.

I am indebted to Faber & Faber Limited for permission to quote from T. S. Eliot's *The Waste Land*.

There are a large number of people to whom I owe a more informal debt for spending their time talking to me on this and allied subjects over the last few years. In particular I need to thank Alistair MacIntosh and Roger Smalley, with or against whom I worked out some of the basic theses; Saul Gellerman, a missionary who realizes his role; Igor Ansoff, Jim Barrett, Carl Duerr, Harry Stieglitz and Bob Tannehill, who nearly succeeded in convincing me that Americans *are* more pragmatic than the British; Dean Berry, for his unwarranted confidence in my ability to write the book; Walter Reid, for so many insights into the mind of the accountant; Ted Riess and Ted Downham, for making me realize that behavioural change and psychiatry were essentially the same; and Martin Brackenbury, the only anthropologist I know of actually working in management.

I also owe much to the management and staff of the Burnham Beeches Hotel; the thinking in this book was shaped a great deal by their excellent cuisine and cellar and the colleagues and friends with whom I shared it.

More about Penguins and Pelicans

Penguinews, which appears every month, contains details of all the new books issued by Penguins as they are published. From time to time it is supplemented by *Penguins in Print*, which is a complete list of all available books published by Penguins. (There are well over four thousand of these.)

A specimen copy of *Penguinews* will be sent to you free on request, and you can become a subscriber for the price of the postage. For a year's issues (including the complete lists) please send 30p if you live in the United Kingdom, or 60p if you live elsewhere. Just write to Dept EP, Penguin Books Ltd, Harmondsworth, Middlesex, enclosing a cheque or postal order, and your name will be added to the mailing list.

Note: *Penguinews* and *Penguins in Print* are not available in the U.S.A. or Canada

Exploration in Management

Wilfred Brown

Few books have made such an impact on our current thinking about business efficiency as *Exploration in Management*, the result of more than twenty years of practical analysis of the central problems of management. In form an account of the application of social study techniques to one large engineering firm, the book is in fact relevant to all those who are concerned in any way with business decisions.

A theory of efficient organization which embraces structure, technique, and human relations is excitingly related to everyday problems from the board-room to the factory floor. The executive role, the manager – surbordinate relationship, the conflict in policy decisions, the representative system, and above all the gaps below the executive system all come under the author's microscope. Lord Brown's unique combination of theory and practice marks out *Exploration in Management* as a permanent contribution for industrialists and social scientists alike.

'His enthusiasm for efficient management, his dedication to the practice of functional application of sound managerial principles come shining through the close web of his reasoning' – Sir Miles Thomas

Not for sale in the U.S.A.

Modern Management Methods

Ernest Dale and L. C. Michelon

Critical path analysis (not forgetting PERT), decision trees, payoff tables, value analysis, operations research ... are these merely samples of the jargon with which the blind blind the blind in business and industry today? Or do the terms describe simple enough and sensible enough methods for coping with complex plans and decisions?

This Pelican provides a very readable and comprehensible introduction to these types of modern technique. In addition the authors offer practical suggestions to directors and managers for planning their own work and running departments; for selecting, training, and getting the best results out of staff, for looking ahead, whether to the introduction of a new product or the installation of a computer; and generally for performing the many functions of good management.

Modern Management Methods is based on the authors' wide experience as management consultants in contact with progressive companies and organizations, and the text of the book (which grew from a closed-circuit television programme) has been thoroughly subjected to the criticism of active managers and re-shaped to meet it.

Not for sale in the U.S.A.